BOB MCLEAN was a founding member of the Campaign for a Scottish Assembly in 1980, served on the National Executive of the CSA/P from 1984 and was latterly a Vice Convener. A former President of the National Union of Students, Scotland, and a member of the Labour Party, he was Convener of Scottish Labour Action, the pro-home rule pressure group.

Dr Bob McLean writes and lectures on aspects of Scottish and Irish history, in particular the Irish War of Independence, the Irish Free State, and the Scottish Labour and Home Rule movements.

I remember meetings in various houses and rooms, the summoning of reserves that led to the setting up of the Constitutional Convention, and that feeling of despair when Labour lost the 1992 general election. I remember the Vigil and acrid smoke from whatever went into the brazier. I also recall months of concern when the Green representatives on the Convention withdrew, over the apparent weakening of the position on proportional representation. The road to victory and the Yes campaign appeared out of those mists.

We should remember all those who did the little things, and celebrate them.

ROBIN HARPER MSP, SCOTTISH GREEN PARTY

The CSA/P was an amazing example of how a small band of enthusiasts with committed leaders such as Jim Boyack can keep a cause alive. It provided a forum to bring together home rulers from several parties and more who would otherwise have sulked in their separate tents after the disaster of 1978/79.

Setting up the committee which composed the Claim of Right, gave the home rule cause renewed legitimacy and appeal and attracted non party-political support. This led to the Constitutional Convention being set up on a broad and co-operative basis when the tide flowed again in favour of home rule.

DONALD GORRIE MSP, SCOTTISH LIBERAL DEMOCRATS

After the 1979 referendum and general election, it would have been easy to walk away from the fight for Scottish democracy. Without the energy and drive of the Campaign for a Scottish Assembly/Parliament, I doubt that the exhilarating victory of September 1997 would ever have been achieved.

On a personal level, without the enthusiasm and commitment of the late Jim Boyack, and his belief in the critical role of the Scottish Labour Party in achieving a Scottish Parliament, I would not hav̶   ̶ur national legislature. It is to people like Jim th̶   ̶e, an ordinary Scot with extraordinary ambitions f̶c̶

FRANK McAVEETY MSP, SCOTTI̶

D1510962

The CSA was a bit of a puzzle for me̶   ̶rmally affiliated to the Campaign, yet Labour Party members like Jim Boyack and Bob McLean were key players in the CSA. It was also odd to sit around the table with

Liberal Democrats, Nationalists and others, but I soon learned that it is important to work with other parties when the occasion demands it.

When the Scottish Parliament convened in May 1999, and when the new building opened in October, my thoughts dwelt on those who carried the CSA/P through difficult times, for example Jim Ross, Alan Lawson and Brian Duncan. As a Labour MSP, I am proud that a Labour government introduced the Scottish home rule settlement. It is also important, however, that the contributions of campaigners, of all parties and none, are recorded.

PAULINE McNEILL MSP, SCOTTISH LABOUR PARTY

When Margaret Thatcher came to power in 1979, one of the first things she did was to repeal the Scotland Act, despite the fact that the majority of Scots had supported home rule in the referendum held earlier that year. During those days the Campaign for a Scottish Assembly was founded. The Campaign had a vital role to play in building the cross party co-operation, which led to the formation of the Scottish Constitutional Convention. The rebirth of our parliament after nearly 300 years is due in no small way to those pioneers who raised the standard and kept it flying throughout all those years of struggle.

DENNIS CANAVAN MSP, INDEPENDENT

In 1979 Labour offered an 'Assembly'. In 1997 the Scottish people voted for a more powerful 'Parliament'. The work of the CSA was crucial to that process with the publication of the Claim of Right and the subsequent blue print developed by the Constitutional Convention. The CSA kept the dream of home rule alive throughout the Tory years. The consensus forged by the Constitutional Convention enabled Donald Dewar to drive the devolution Whitepaper through Whitehall without it being 'watered down' or derailed.

The Scottish Parliament is here to stay. Our challenge is to deliver the promise that energised generations of home rulers.

SARAH BOYACK MSP, SCOTTISH LABOUR PARTY

While the glory days of the Campaign for a Scottish Parliament might seem to be around the achievement of devolution in the late 1990s, the real heroes were the campaigners of the 1980s.

After the demoralisation of 1979, the then Campaign for a Scottish Assembly was a brave attempt to keep the flame burning and recover unity in the home rule ranks. The small but determined group who kept the potential of devolution on the political agenda laid the ground for the historic events of 1999.

The establishment of a committee under Sir Robert Grieve, the persuasion of pro-devolution forces to join a Constitutional Convention and the success of that Convention were real landmarks. Jim Boyack and the others – from all parties – who put in so much effort and commitment should never be forgotten. That is why I welcome this publication which will ensure that the CSP will live on in Scotland's political history.

RT HON JACK McCONNELL MSP
FIRST MINISTER OF SCOTLAND

Getting it Together

The History of the Campaign for a Scottish Assembly/Parliament 1980–1999

BOB McLEAN

Luath Press Limited

EDINBURGH

www.luath.co.uk

First published 2005

The paper used in this book is recyclable. It is made from
low-chlorine pulps produced in a low-energy, low-emission manner
from renewable forests.

Printed and bound by
DigiSource (GB) Ltd., Livingston

Typeset in 12 point Sabon by
S. Fairgrieve, Edinburgh 0131 658 1763

GETTING IT TOGETHER was a favourite catch phrase coined by the late Jim Boyack. As Convener of the Campaign for a Scottish Assembly/ Parliament, Jim held the organisation together during difficult and frustrating times. This book is dedicated to his memory, and to the efforts of all of those campaigned for a Scottish Assembly, or Parliament, with such powers as desired by the people of Scotland.

Contents

Introduction

IN THE EAST END of Edinburgh's city centre is the busy junction where the thoroughfares of Broughton Street, Picardy Place, York Place and Greenside Place converge. It is an area rich in landmarks to Scottish identity and creativity. Picardy Place takes its name from the French craftsmen who were settled there in the 18th century to 'wrocht for the Linen Company'. Nearby, the statue of a familiar caped, pipe-smoking crime fighter marks the site of Number 11 Picardy Place, the birthplace of Sir Arthur Conan Doyle, the Scottish creator of the great London detective modelled on an Edinburgh medic. The junction is dominated by St Mary's Roman Catholic Metropolitan Cathedral, a status awarded to that ancient place of worship to mark the restoration of Scotland's Catholic hierarchy in 1878, reflecting the impact of later immigrants, from Ireland and Italy, in the mid to late 19th century. In more recent times the precinct of the Cathedral has been enhanced by street sculpture created by one of Leith and Scotland's favourite Italian/Scottish sons, Sir Edwardo Paolozzi.

Picardy Place also houses the headquarters of the Edinburgh and District Trades Council, and it was in the former social club of that organisation that some 400 men and women gathered on Saturday 1 March 1980. They met to mark the first anniversary of the indecisive referendum on Scottish devolution. They had not come to bury the aspiration to Scottish home rule, but to revive it through the creation of a cross-party, single-issue pressure group, the Campaign for a Scottish Assembly.

Almost exactly nineteen years later, members of the organisation, then styled the Campaign for a Scottish Parliament, met for the last time on Saturday 29 March 1999, just a matter of weeks before the first ever democratic elections to Scotland's Parliament. One of the decisions taken at that final gathering was that I should compile an 'official' history of the Campaign and its contribution to winning Scotland's Parliament. My credentials for undertaking the exercise are my involvement with the Campaign. I was present at the founding rally in Edinburgh on 1 March 1980, but it was from 1984 onwards that I joined the National Executive and became centrally involved with the Campaign. In establishing my 'bona fides' I should also lodge a couple of caveats. Throughout the period under review I was very active in Labour Party affairs, particularly the development of Labour policy on home rule. It would only be natural if that orientation is reflected in this account. Throughout, however, I have consciously sought to avoid any Labour bias.

It is also important to make the scope of this study very clear. There are several books on the road to Scottish home rule and the battle for a Scottish Parliament. The purpose of this account is to record and evaluate the contribution of one of the organisations campaigning for Scottish home rule. In particular I examine:

- the formation of the Campaign and the nurturing of the home rule dream during the very difficult years between 1979 and 1987

- the inter-relationship between the CSA/CSP and the Scottish Constitutional Convention in the period 1988 to 1997

En route, I examine the organisation of the CSA/CSP, its finances, campaigns and base of support. While I have maintained a relatively narrow focus on the CSA/CSP, I have set the Campaign in the historical context of earlier Scottish home rule pressure groups. I have also commented on wider aspects of the Scottish question where I regard other accounts to be incomplete or inaccurate.

Throughout, I have drawn from primary sources wherever possible, and I thank all those former members of the CSA/CSP who passed their own files on to me. I owe a particular debt to the comprehensive collection of CSA/CSP documents held by the Gallacher Memorial Library at Glasgow Caledonian University, thanks to the meticulous care of Audrey and Eric Canning. It is my intention to deposit the papers in my possession with the National Library of Scotland. That should provide two centres of CSA/CSP archives, one in Glasgow, the other in Edinburgh.

I hope that the manuscript will be of interest to students of the period, those interested in the study of pressure group politics and those who were directly involved.

Returning to the clutch of landmarks, statues and shrines at the top of Leith Walk, there is a strong case for the birthplace of the CSA/CSP to be recognised in some way. In the meantime, this manuscript is offered as a tribute to the men and women of the CSA/CSP who campaigned for Scottish democracy over two decades.

CHAPTER I

Conventions all Round

The modern Campaign for a Scottish Assembly/Parliament in the context of earlier Scottish home rule pressure groups

In the Beginning

BURNS WROTE THAT THE incorporating Union of 1707 was 'wrought by a coward few', without any heed for popular opinion nor endorsement. Before long, however, the 'parcel of rogues' that had stitched the deal were on their feet at Westminster, outraged at Treaty infringements which interfered with Scottish church affairs and threatened Scottish commerce. Elite disillusion with the Union was restrained, however, by fear of the return of the Stuart dynasty. By the time that scenario had ceased to be a serious threat, in the 1750s, the hopes for commercial benefits of the Union were beginning to materialise. The fortunes accrued by tobacco and cotton barons greased the wheels of the Industrial Revolution, and the development of the iron, coal and shipbuilding industries. Abandoned by the ruling elite, the torch of Scottish national sentiment was picked up by those who were influenced by the democratic rhetoric and ideals of the American and French revolutions.

One of the most notable figures to step forward was radical lawyer Thomas Muir who called from French exile for the establishment of a Scottish Republic, with himself at the head of a 'Scotch Directory'.[1] While Muir languished in Chantilly, sections of his supporters at home, the United Scotsmen, turned to direct action in pursuit of democratic and national rights, inspired, at the name suggests, by Wolf Tone's United Irishmen. Following the Napoleonic Wars commemoration rallies lauding Bruce and Wallace were effectively a front for democratic demonstrations and *Scots Wha Hae* was adopted as the Scottish radical anthem.[2] The 400 or so Scottish radicals who marched into the Insurrection of 1820 did so under the banner of 'Scotland Free or a Desert'.[3]

The banners carried and the medallions struck in the campaigns that resulted in the Reform Acts of 1832 and 1867, linked national and democratic demands by calling for 'Scottish Rights' and 'Democracy for Scotland'. It is only after the 'third' Reform Act of 1884, however, that it is possible to talk of mass democratic politics. From the Union to the 1820s, Scotland was managed as a pocket burgh with a tiny electorate. The 1832 Reform Act extended the Scottish electorate from 4,500 to 65,000. Following the 1884 Act, 40% of all Scottish adult males, and 100% of Scottish women, were still denied the vote. With the male heads of all households enfranchised, however, it paved the way for the kind of home rule pressure group politics in which the Campaign for a Scottish Assembly/Parliament of the 1980s and '90s was firmly anchored.

The first movement on the British mainland to take advantage of the changing political landscape was the Highland Land League or 'Crofters' Party'. Keen students of the fortunes of the Irish Land League, and the Irish Parliamentary Party, the Scottish highlanders and islanders learned the key lesson. Ordinary people could advance their collective interests by the disciplined application of their combined political clout. At the general elections of 1885 and 1886 the Crofters elected five representatives to advocate their case at Westminster.

The immediate demands of the Scottish Crofters were based around 'the three Fs': fixity of tenure, fair rents and the freedom to inherit holdings. The shared grievances of Highland crofter and Irish tenant farmer produced a crypto celtic nationalism.[4] Between 1886 and 1893, the Crofters' leader at Westminster, Dr. Gavin B. Clark, moved five separate Scottish home rule bills. In 1886 Clark was a founding member, and Vice President, of the Scottish Home Rule Association, the direct precursor of the CSA/CSP.

The Original Scottish Home Rule Association

The original Scottish Home Rule Association (SHRA), founded in 1886, published pamphlets, issued appeals to the Scots diaspora in the dominions and supported candidates for public office who were known to favour home rule. The major beneficiaries of that support were those on the Gladstonian wing of the Liberal Party. The SHRA was heavily dominated by active Liberals. It has been argued that the Association was effectively an internal Liberal Party pressure group, promoting Scottish home rule as a means of squaring Gladstone's attempts to introduce Irish home rule.[5] This is borne out by SHRA statements such as:

'the question of Home Rule would be more easily solved if the cases of Ireland and Scotland were taken together.'[6]

and:

'Scottish Home Rule has made the Irish movement respectable.'[7]

In 1888, however, the SHRA supported the independent labour candidature of another of its Vice Presidents, James Keir Hardie, in the Mid-Lanark parliamentary by election. Several leading members of the Association were active in the Mid-Lanark by election, although they tended to be better known as Crofters' MPs, local trade union leaders or members of socialist societies. Official SHRA support for Hardie came from Ramsay MacDonald, who sent him best wishes in his capacity as Secretary of the London Branch of the Association. It was an early communication between two future leaders of the Labour Party.

If the original Scottish Home Rule Association was federalist, it was also very loyal to the imperial connection. One of the posts on its large Executive was that of 'Colonial Secretary'.[8] The aims and objectives of the Association committed it to 'sacredly maintaining the unity and supremacy' of Westminster to 'manage all imperial affairs'.[9] From its pamphlets and pronouncements, however, it appears that the Association had difficulties in distinguishing between 'national' and 'imperial' affairs. While the Association welcomed supportive

MPs moving home rule bills at Westminster, much of the would-be legislation was light on detail. So much so that John Ferguson, one of the first leaders of the Irish community in Scotland to break with Liberalism for nascent Labour, described proto-legislation as 'unscientific jumble'.[10]

Calls for a Convention

It may have been the lack of definition of exactly what 'home rule' meant that prompted Association Treasurer, William Mitchell, to propose to the 1892 conference of the SHRA that the Association should call for the establishment of a constitutional convention, or more accurately, conventions. Mitchell argued that the best way to arrive at a stable constitutional settlement was for Westminster to list the 'legislative and administrative functions' that could possibly be devolved to home rule parliaments, and to convene Scottish, Irish, Welsh and English constitutional conventions which would meet and agree 'such constitutions as each country may consider most suitable for the legislature of its own division'.[11]

The opposition to Mitchell's proposal was led by Keir Hardie, who successfully argued that it was the job of Scottish MPs to draw up an acceptable home rule scheme.[12]

While Mitchell's proposal for 'conventions all round' was rejected, and the Association gradually faded from the political scene in the late 1890s, the Original SHRA is the earliest example of a broad movement campaigning for Scottish home rule in the democratic era. It also pointed to the historic examples of American and French representative conventions in agreeing the details of constitutional change.

The Young Scots

While the Liberal grandees of the 1880s and '90s may have regarded Scottish home rule as an expedient, to rectify the anomalies raised by Irish autonomy, there is no doubt about the priority accorded to it by a new generation of Liberal activists – the Young Scots. The manifesto issued by this internal Liberal pressure group in 1911 advocated a radical 'New Liberalism' embracing land reform, poor law reform, public housing and increased access to education. At the heart of their programme was a commitment to Scottish home rule, which they described as 'the most urgent reform of the time'.[13]

Although the outbreak of World War 1 in 1914 was the end of the Young Scots, and although it was an internal party pressure group, it is worthy of mention in this context as it witnessed the emergence of Roland Eugene Muirhead. Muirhead's organisational ability and political stamina saw him remain at the centre of campaigns for Scottish home rule for more than fifty years.

The War Years

The great power tensions, which led to a war to defend the rights of small nations, prompted some home rulers to take advantage of the situation in an attempt to bring international pressure to bear on the Liberal government to introduce home rule for Scotland. Founded in 1913, the International Scots Home Rule League, led by the Marquess of Graham and including a young Roland Muirhead, sought to influence the outcome of two pre-war by elections, but as the world descended into war the organisation faded from the scene.

The most significant development during the war years was the transformation of the situation in Ireland. The events that followed the Easter Rising of 1916 had by late 1918 rendered a solution based on pre-war legislative models obsolete, and with them the concept of 'home rule all round'.

Developments in Ireland weakened the links between the Irish in Scotland and the Liberal Party, which pre-war Scottish Labour pioneers had found so difficult to break. Increasingly deserted by their Irish supporters, the Liberal Party was badly wounded by Lloyd George's National Liberal breakaway. Labour also benefited from an increased electorate, sections of which had been radicalised by the war.

In 1916 and 1918 the Scottish Trades Union Congress endorsed earlier resolutions in favour of Scottish home rule, and in 1916 the Scottish Advisory Council of the Labour Party officially embraced the pro-home rule faith of the Scottish Labour pioneers.

The 'Second' Scottish Home Rule Association

Labour in Scotland fought the November 1918 general election as the standard bearer of home rule. The anticipated electoral breakthrough was postponed to 1922 as the electorate rewarded the War time Coalition. Electoral disappointment prompted extra-parliamentary campaigning, and Muirhead, by then a member of the Labour Party, called a meeting of veteran and influential home rulers to discuss the creation of a new pressure group.[14] On 29 March 1919 the reformed, or 'second' Scottish Home Rule Association held its inaugural conference.[15] Muirhead was elected as its Secretary.

R.E. Muirhead

Roland Eugene Muirhead had an interesting radical pedigree. Born in Renfrewshire in 1868 he belonged to a family with its own tannery business. His uncle, Henry, had campaigned for women's admission to Scottish universities, his sister Margaret was a prominent suffragette, and his older brother, Robert, was a socialist pioneer who introduced the young Roland to Keir Hardie and Cunninghame Graham.

As a young man, Muirhead travelled widely and for a period worked and lived in a co-operative community in Washington State in the USA. Returning to Scotland in 1892, Muirhead re-organised the family firm along co-operative lines, introducing a 40 hour working week. He returned convinced that Scotland could run her domestic affairs. In 1901 he joined the Young Scots. In 1906 he helped Tom Johnston launch 'Forward', the journal of the Independent Labour Party in Scotland, and in 1918 Muirhead joined both the ILP and the Labour Party. Muirhead was very shy and no great orator, but he was the ultimate backroom boy.[16]

While the second Scottish Home Rule Association attracted the involvement of many Labour figures, and the affiliation of many trade union and party organisations, the Party at Scottish level was more wary. In 1919 the Conference of the Scottish Advisory Council of the Labour Party resolved:

'...the people of Scotland can secure this measure (home rule) by a fuller support of Labour at the polls, and therefore considers it inadvisable for members of the Labour Party to associate with members of other political parties in special organisations for the purpose of securing home rule...'[17]

As the CSA was to discover in the 1980s, there was an ingrained suspicion of co-operating with others in the pursuit of Scottish democracy in some corners of Labour officialdom.

'Changed Utterly'

One major difference in the political landscape facing the second SHRA was the Anglo/Irish Treaty, which bestowed enhanced dominion status on the 26 counties of nationalist Ireland. As the SHRA newsletter put it:

'The Irish settlement has put Federal Home Rule, as hitherto understood, out of practical politics.'[18]

Attempts to demand dominion status for Scotland were rejected by the SHRA amid concern that any settlement which might threaten the future presence of Scottish MPs at Westminster would divide the Association.[19] The SHRA defined its position as follows:

'... any scheme for Scottish self-government should first secure the approval of a National Convention of the people of Scotland, to be called at an early date, and while prepared to submit its own provisional scheme, the Association does not aim at dictating the details of such a scheme to the coming National Convention.'[20]

The concept of determining Scotland's constitutional future via a constitutional convention, discussed but rejected by the 'first' Scottish Home Rule Association, had now become the policy of the 'second' SHRA. It was a strategy that later cross-party home rule groups, including the CSA/CSP, would return to.

Labour Breaks Through

In the general election of 1922, Labour increased its representation to 29 seats, making it the largest single party in Scotland. The indecisive result through the United Kingdom as a whole promised another election in a matter of months. In 1923 Labour increased its seats to 35 and formed a minority government at Westminster. Labour's Scottish Parliamentary Group contained a number of leading figures, mainly members of the Independent Labour Party, who had strong records on the home rule issue. Thanks to the private member's bill procedure, it fell to one of their number, George Buchanan, to introduce a home rule bill.

Buchanan's Bill

Buchanan met with officers of the SHRA but they could not agree on the contents of the bill. Buchanan opposed the convention proposal, as Hardie had done in 1892. If the SHRA could not command agreement in its own ranks, what prospect of a convention reaching consensus? Buchanan also made it clear to the SHRA that he would not advocate anything that might undermine continuing Scottish representation at Westminster.[21]

George Buchanan's bill was based closely on the 1914 Government of Ireland Act. On the question of Scottish representation at Westminster, it proposed no change until home rule was introduced for England and Wales, at which point the entire composition of the House of Commons could be reviewed.[22]

The bill received a second reading on 9 May 1924, and was seconded by Tom Johnston. When the time allocated for debate expired, the Speaker created uproar by refusing to call a vote. He based his ruling on the grounds that there were still Scottish members, Unionists, wishing to speak. MacDonald's minority government rejected proposals to allocate additional parliamentary time to the bill, and to refer it to a Royal Commission or select committee. Buchanan's Bill had failed.[23]

Given Labour's support for home rule, the formation of the first

Labour Government convinced campaigners that a Scottish Parliament would be along in a tick. The debacle surrounding Buchanan's Bill shook that confidence. Home rule bills had failed in the past, but never before had expectations been so high. The frustrations created by the failure of the bill are illustrated in the sharp exchanges between hitherto collaborators Muirhead and Johnston. Muirhead maintained that MacDonald's government should have allocated additional time. Johnston argued that during May, June and July 1924, the government had presented legislation on employment, insurance, housing, agricultural wages and a budget. Parliament was in recess during August and September, and in October 1924 the first Labour government fell.[24] The 1924 general election, the 'Zinoviev Letter' election, returned a massive Conservative and Unionist majority to Westminster.

Return to Convention

With the prospect of progress at Westminster blocked for the duration, the SHRA concentrated on its policy on a convention. When a convention was first held in November 1924, it was supported by eight MPs, twenty eight local authorities and the Convention of Scottish Royal Burghs, a forerunner of the modern COSLA. The first full meeting of the Scottish National Convention elected a committee charged with preparing a draft home rule scheme to be placed before a reconvened meeting.[25] In the 1990s there was concern that the Scottish Constitutional Convention took more than eighteen months, from March 1989 to November 1990, to produce its first report. That timetable mirrors almost exactly the time taken by the Scottish National Convention's drafting committee to complete its remit. In the interregnum, discussions took place within the SHRA as to whether or not the creation of an independent nationalist party would force the pace on constitutional change. Such talk subsided with the publication of the drafting committee's report in July 1926 and the second meeting of the full Convention in October.[26]

The home rule scheme approved by the Scottish National Convention addressed the 'English problem', the issue which in more modern times came to be known as the 'West Lothian Question'. Under the

National Convention scheme, Scottish MPs would withdraw from Westminster and defence, foreign affairs, and other 'imperial matters' would be the responsibility of an Imperial Council on which Scotland would be represented by its home rule government. This suggestion ensured that the scheme was rejected by Westminster, on two occasions, and easily sidelined.[27] Critics attacked the 1990s Constitutional Convention scheme for avoiding the West Lothian Question. The fate of the 1920s National Convention suggests that to have done otherwise would have narrowed its base of support and made consensus more difficult to achieve.

Towards an Independent Nationalist Party

The failure of the Scottish National Convention unleashed latent divisions within the Scottish Home Rule Association. In May 1928 Muirhead and Association President Robert Bontine Cunninghame Graham, committed themselves to an independent nationalist party. Without Muirhead's organisational skills and financial backing, the 'second' Scottish Home Rule Association went into decline. At the Association's annual general meeting on 13 April 1929 the remnants of the SHRA carried the following resolution:

'the time has come when the activities of the Scottish Home Association should cease, and its affairs wound up.'[28]

The inaugural rally of the National Party of Scotland was held in Stirling on Saturday 23 June 1928.[29] The platform included Glasgow University student leader, John MacCormick, and the chair was taken by the party's first president, Cunninghame Graham. Almost forty years earlier Cunninghame Graham had played the same role at the founding conference of the Scottish Labour Party. It befalls few people to play a central role in the formation of one major political party, never mind two!

The Uncrowned King of Scots

To his Perthshire tenants he was 'Gartmore', to the gauchos of the Pampas 'Don Roberto', to the early socialist pioneers 'comrade'. Robert Cunninghame Graham was born in London in 1852, heir to two of Scotland's oldest families, the Cunninghame Earls of Glencairn and the Graham Earls of Menteith. One of his forebears fought alongside Wallace at Falkirk, and, through the Menteith line, he could claim illegitimate descent from King Robert II, a connection that prompted the antiquarian Andrew Lang to dub him the 'Uncrowned King of Scots'.

From his Spanish maternal grandmother the young Robert inherited a passion for Spanish culture. This led to travels in South America and, when still a teenager, he won the respect of the hard riding gauchos of Argentina. Later he lived with native Amercian Indians in Mexico where he befriended William Cody, better known as 'Buffalo Bill'.

Cunninghame Graham returned from his travels convinced that Scotland could only benefit from greater control over her own affairs. On the Radical wing of the Liberal Party, he was elected as the MP for North West Lanark in 1886. At Westminster he supported the demands of the Crofters' Party and campaigned for an eight hour working day in the mining industry, a struggle which brought him into contact with Keir Hardie.[30] In 1888 he supported Hardie's labour candidature at Mid Lanark, and later that year he became the first president of the Scottish Labour Party. A close friend of the Irish-born Glasgow Boy, Sir John Lavery, Cunninghame Graham continued to travel and in later life became better known for his writings based on his wanderings.

A vice president of the original Scottish Home Rule Association in the 1880s, he served as president of the 'second' SHRA in the 1920s. The first president of the National Party of Scotland, he came to within 66 votes of defeating Prime Minister Stanley Baldwin in an election for the Rectorship of the University of Glasgow.

Cunninghame Graham's long and colourful life came to an end in 1936, age 84. He lies buried on the island of Inchmahon on the Lake of Menteith.[31]

A Marker on the Future

From the 1880s to the late 1920s, more than twenty Scottish home rule bills were moved and defeated, or stalled, at Westminster. The bills moved by the Reverend James Barr, in 1927 and 1928, were of particular significance as they were based on the work of a representative gathering in Scotland – the Scottish National Convention. The calling of a convention to devise a consensus home rule scheme is not the only similarity between the SHRA of the 1920s and the Campaign for a Scottish Assembly/Parliament in the 1980s and '90s.

Both organisations produced regular newsletters, and publications on various aspects of the home rule question. Both organisations rallied on significant dates. For the SHRA it tended to be 20 June and 30 November, while 1 March was preferred by the CSA/P. Both organisations lobbied political candidates and sought to ensure the success of those committed to home rule. At the height of its popularity the SHRA reached 3,000 individual members and 300 affiliated organisations.[32] While those numbers are greater than those achieved by the CSA/CSP, they are in the same ballpark, particularly when the downturn in political activism in more recent times is taken into account. The list of organisations affiliated to the SHRA looks pretty similar to those associated with the CSA/CSP. It included Labour Party organisations, Liberal Party organisations, trades unions, trades councils, cultural organisations, and the Co-operative movement.[33]

Both the SHRA and the CSA/CSP were indebted to key individuals who invested their energy, time, and, in certain cases, money. The SHRA had Muirhead, Cunninghame Graham and Gallagher. The CSA/P had Jim Boyack, Hugh Miller, Isobel Lindsay, Jim Ross, Alan Lawson and many more.

While political movements in the UK, other than major political parties, may sparkle for a moment, they soon fade away without the last rites ever being administered. Both the SHRA and the CSA/CSP formally dissolved themselves, but that is where the similarities end. The SHRA wound itself up in April 1929 against a background of division and uncertainty, with no realistic prospect of its goal being achieved in the medium term. When the CSA/CSP met to dissolve on a fine spring morning almost exactly 70 years later, the campaign was already underway for the first ever democratic elections to a Scottish Parliament.

The Covenant Movement: The Cold Dawn of Reality

John MacCormick and his Glasgow University Scottish Nationalist Association was central to the birth of the National Party of Scotland, and death of the Scottish Home Rule Association. The environ of Glasgow University was the arena for the new party's first contest when Cunninghame Graham came so close to embarrassing Prime Minister Baldwin in the election for Rector. It was only a matter of weeks, however, before the NPS encountered reality. The setting was my own neck of the woods, the North Midlothian by election of January 1929. The National Party candidate was the poet Lewis Spence and he could count on some pretty impressive support. At a public meeting in Dalkeith's Corn Exchange, Spence's platform was elevated by the presence of Muirhead, Cunninghame Graham, C.M. Grieve (Hugh MacDiarmid) and John MacCormick.[34] Despite a spirited campaign, Spence trailed last behind local miners' agent, David Clarke, with just 4% of the vote.[35] The result was a shock to those who thought that pro-home rule sentiment would translate into votes for the NPS. This initial disappointing result was borne out in the general election a few months later.

Independent nationalism ploughed a fallow field through the 1930s, and the outbreak of war brought divisions born of disappointment and frustration to the fore. The ranks of what became the Scottish National Party in 1934 were divided over their attitudes to World War II, the electoral truce observed by the major parties and working with others to secure change at war's end. The strains broke out into the open at the SNP's 1942 Conference. Paradoxically, it was John MacCormick who emerged as the leader of a pluralist strand which backed the war effort, respected the truce and had an open attitude to working with other people. MacCormick and his supporters formed Scottish Convention.[36]

Scottish Convention

The central policy of Scottish Convention was the creation of a representative assembly, the Scottish National Assembly, which, like the SHRA's Scottish National Convention of 1925-28, would seek consensus around a home rule scheme. The first Assembly gathered on 27 March 1947 against a background of rising Scottish sentiment.

While the achievements of the post-war Labour government continue to be lauded today, they should not conceal the fact that many of the reforms and new institutions were organised on a highly centralist model, and there was a perception that control and decision making were being removed from Scotland. Interestingly, the STUC and many Scottish Labour MPs were concerned that the regulation of air traffic control in 1946 made no provision for a Scottish authority.[37] Insensitivity to Scottish aspirations was one of the factors leading the STUC to reaffirm its support for home rule at its 1947 Conference. The 1940s also witnessed the advent of scientific opinion polling on the home rule question. The first such poll, conducted for the *Edinburgh Evening News* in November 1945, found 75% in favour of some form of home rule. A poll in the *Daily Express* the following year placed support at a remarkably similar 76%.[38]

The Scottish National Assembly

Some 400 delegates assembled in the Christian Institute in Glasgow for the first meeting of the Scottish National Assembly. The councils of Glasgow, Aberdeen, Paisley and Greenock were represented as were a further 36 town or burgh councils and 16 district or county councils. There were delegates from churches, trade unions, chambers of commerce, co-operative societies, a smattering of peers and a few MPs.[39] MacCormick, by that point a member of the Liberal Party, took the chair, and the opening statement was delivered by Scottish Convention's Vice President, Co-op leader William Gallagher, who embodied a direct link with the SHRA of the 1920s. The other Willie Gallacher, the Communist MP, attended and addressed the Assembly. The man who had fought with John MacLean over the Scottish

Question squared up to the accusation of being 'a one time revolutionary turned Scottish nationalist'.[40]

Following the break with MacLean, the Communist Party of Great Britain remained dismissive of home rule, but that opposition was dropped during the 'popular front' period. In 1948 the Scottish Committee of the CPGB published John Gollan's *Scottish Prospect,* which set the Party on the home rule road.[41]

Other speakers from the floor of the Assembly included David Gibson, representing the rump of the old Independent Labour Party, and Douglas Young of the SNP.[42] One of the features that distinguished the National Assembly of 1947 from the National Convention of the 1920s, and the Constitutional Convention of the 1990s, was the presence of Conservatives, eager to exploit unease at the centralising effect of the government's policies. Colonel Gomme-Duncan, one of five Tory MPs present, called for an end to Scotland being treated as 'an office boy', while Tory peers the Earl of Selkirk and Lord Polworth both called for the establishment of a Royal Commission on Scotland's constitutional future. So much for the Communists, Liberals, ILP, SNP and the Tory Unionists, but what about the Labour Party? Of the two Labour MPs present only one spoke, and she stopped short of supporting a Scottish Parliament.[43]

The first meeting of the Scottish National Assembly concluded by electing a committee of 35 people, to produce a draft home rule scheme within a year. But before the second meeting of the National Assembly convened in March of 1948, events intervened which seriously damaged the Scottish Convention project.

John MacCormick

John MacCormick was from a middle class Argyllshire background. He joined the student Labour Club on arriving at the University of Glasgow in 1925. An outstanding debater, MacCormick was talent-spotted by the ILP/Labour Party and in the summer of 1927 he was dispatched on a speaking tour of rural Argyll with the Labour prospective parliamentary candidate. According to his autobiography, MacCormick found his companion's lack of confidence in Labour's ability to deliver on home rule less than inspiring, and on his return to University he formed the Scottish Nationalist Association, and is credited with forcing the pace in the formation of the National Party of Scotland.[44]

Frustrated by NPS/SNP lack of electoral success, MacCormick reversed his position and in 1942 led the breakaway Scottish Convention on a gradualist platform. Having quit the SNP, MacCormick joined the Liberal Party, a move that complimented Scottish Convention's approach to home rule. In the course of 1947 he was selected as the Liberal prospective parliamentary candidate for Paisley.

The Paisley By Election

In December 1947 former Tory Prime Minister, Stanley Baldwin died, thereby elevating his son, Viscount Corvedale, the Labour MP for Paisley, to the House of Lords. Following considerable lobbying and intrigue MacCormick contested the by election as 'National' candidate, jointly endorsed by the local Liberals, the Unionists, the National Liberal Party and a smattering of SNP members.[45]

As someone seeking to build a cross-party campaign for home rule, MacCormick's actions in ganging up against Labour, Scotland's largest party and the party of government, were a massive miscalculation. MacCormick argued that the Tories, crushed in 1945, were looking for a new big idea, and wanted to position themselves as the party of local control, as opposed to Labour's centralism. To MacCormick it was an opportunity to lead Toryism along the decentralist path to Scottish home rule.[46]

MacCormick's manifesto, or 'declaration', listed Scottish home rule as its seventh policy point, and Labour scented a plot to unite the right against the left. MacCormick fuelled that fear with his comment that he hoped the by election would split the Labour Party and isolate the left.[47] Although Labour's Douglas Johnstone defeated MacCormick by 27,213 to 20,668 votes, Paisley confirmed Labour suspicions about Scottish Convention. It also fuelled a paranoia within Scottish Labour culture that would lead to the party regarding the home rule question as a Tory Trojan Horse, and to Labour formally renouncing its home rule inheritance in 1958.

'Blue Print for Scotland'

Within weeks of the Paisley poll, the second meeting of the Scottish National Assembly convened on 20 March 1948 and endorsed the report of the drafting committee. The 'Blue Print for Scotland' harked back to a definition of 'imperial', as opposed to domestic, issues. Considerable attention was directed to the question of Scottish representation at Westminster post-home rule. While the scheme drafted by the Scottish National Convention in the 1920s had honestly attempted to solve the question, the 'Blue Print' approved by the Scottish National Assembly of the late 1940s postponed the issue. It argued that the matter should be dealt with by a Joint Commission of the Westminster and Scottish parliaments, once working experience of home rule had been gained.[48] Interestingly, the CSA/CSP borrowed the title 'Blue Print for Scotland' on two occasions, in the 1980s and 1990s.

The National Covenant

The 'Blue Print for Scotland' agreed, Scottish Convention sought a meeting with government but were denied access to both Downing Street and St. Andrew's House. If the government refused to consider the National Assembly's proposals, perhaps they would respond to a demonstration of public opinion. In October 1949 the third meeting of the National Assembly agreed to launch the National Covenant, a monster petition designed to demonstrate the depth of support in Scotland for home rule.

The National Covenant is a landmark in the history of pressure group campaigning. Within a week of its launch it had been signed by fifty thousand people, and by one million within six months.[49] The total number of signatures reached two million by 1952. Signing the Covenant took off, but who was responsible for the initiative? Scottish Convention had convened the National Assembly. The Assembly supported the launch of the Covenant, and appointed a National

Covenant Committee to oversee it. In an attempt to rationalise this plethora of titles, Scottish Convention and the National Covenant Committee merged to form the Scottish Covenant Association, with membership set at one shilling. MacCormick claimed that the merged organisation had 35,000 members at the height of its powers in 1952.

If this figure is even half correct, the Scottish Covenant Association was the largest ever home rule, cross-party, pressure group. It may be the case that those signing the Covenant regarded the shilling as a donation, rather than a membership subscription. The available membership figures for Scottish Convention, just short of 5,000, are more in keeping with the 1920's Scottish Home Rule Association, and the 1980s/'90s CSA/CSP.[50] Those active in the CSA/CSP in the 1990s will appreciate the confusion that can arise between the role of a campaigning organisation and a convention established to work on a home rule scheme.

Before long the Scottish Covenant Association ran into the problem that will inevitably bedevil any campaign group organised around a single tactic, particularly when government simply refuses to engage.

With another general election likely in 1951, the Labour Government had to be careful in handling the demand for a Scottish Parliament. Accordingly, the newly appointed Secretary of State for Scotland ordered an inquiry to establish, or otherwise, Scotland's alleged financial self-sufficiency.[51]

Keen to take advantage of the pre-election climate to breathe life into the Covenant Strategy, the SCA launched a second petition in the summer of 1951. The 'Declaration' called on all sitting Scottish MPs to pledge to support the establishment of a Royal Commission on Scottish Home Rule after the election. Where a sitting MP refused to sign, the opportunity would pass to the candidate of the party who had come second in the constituency at the 1950 election. The Scottish people were called on to declare that they would support candidates committed to supporting the creation of the Royal Commission proposal.[52] The New Covenanters argued that they were applying pressure where it counted but as the Scottish Unionist Party had already pledged to support a Royal Commission, they were accused of meddling in party politics. With only four exceptions, angry Scottish Labour MPs refused to sign, and only one Labour MP defied a prohibition on attending the fifth and final meeting of the National Assembly in June 1953. The meeting was poorly attended and the organisers were criticised for allowing the Covenant to be undermined by bogus and frivolous signatures. Indecisive rancour broke out over whether or not the Scottish Covenant Association should field candidates in elections.[53]

John MacCormick died in 1961. The Scottish Covenant Association limped on to 1963 but its moment had come, and passed, in 1952.

In from the Cold

Back in power, the Conservatives soon curtailed their flirtation with Scottish home rule. With Labour abandoning its home rule traditions, and the SNP still firmly marooned in the electoral doldrums, the 1950s were a highpoint of 'North British' politics.

The notion of 'never having had it so good' came to an abrupt stop in the mid 1960s. The Tories, who obtained their best ever share of the Scottish vote in 1955, started the slide fashioned by social change and a decline in religious-based voting. Harold Wilson's Labour Government proved popular in Scotland. Support for the ship building industry, the creation of the Highlands and Islands Development Board and a national plan for Scotland were rewarded with a record 46 Scottish seats at the 1966 general election. Within months of the election, however, a sterling crisis led to the collapse of Labour's economic policy, causing closures and unemployment in Scotland's heavy industries, and a contraction in services to rural Scotland. This produced a nascent national sentiment but it did not result in the resurgence of a broad based home rule pressure group. It sought expression elsewhere.[54]

The SNP's 18% in the Glasgow Bridgeton by election in 1961, and the 10,000 votes polled by Billy Wolfe against a young Tam Dalyell in West Lothian a year later, suggested the SNP's ability to move in from the political fringe. The breakthrough came in 1967/68 with 28% in the Glasgow Pollock by election, Winnie Ewing's victory in Hamilton in November 1967, and a net gain of 103 seats in the 1968 municipal elections.

Ted Heath rushed to Perth to declare that devolution of some sort was still on the Tory agenda. Harold Wilson established a Royal Commission on the Constitution. This initiative bought the desired political space but in February 1974 the SNP, buoyed by the discovery of North Sea oil, returned seven MPs. Governing without a majority, Wilson spent the summer persuading Scottish Labour to rediscover its home rule traditions. In October 1974 the SNP increased its parliamentary representation to 11. This was achieved at the expense of the Tories, and Wilson sneaked back into Downing Street with a tiny majority.

Labour's efforts to legislate for their promised Scottish Assembly dominated events at Westminster from 1974-79. The political snakes and ladders game played at Westminster during those years was reminiscent of Gladstone's dealings with Parnell and the Irish Parliamentary Party in the 1880s. For Gladstone and Wilson/Callaghan, delivering on home rule was essential to the survival of their administrations, yet they had to deal with agnosticism and outright opposition on their own backbenches.[55]

NOTES AND REFERENCES

[1] See Henry Meikle, *Scotland and the French Revolution*, 1912
[2] T.C. Smout, *A Century of the Scottish People*, 1986, pp.236-237
[3] For an account of the Radical War, see Peter Berresford Ellis and Seumas Mac A'Ghobhain, *The Scottish Insurrection of 1820*, 1969
[4] See *The Scottish Historical Review*, Vol.35, 1956, 'The Crofters' Party 1885-1892'
[5] See James Mitchell, *Strategies for Self-Government. The Campaigns for a Scottish Parliament*, Polygon, Edinburgh, 1996
[6] Dr Gavin Clarke's presidential address to the 1892 Annual Conference of the Scottish Home Rule Association, quoted in the *Scotsman*, 4 June 1892, p.9
[7] William Mitchell, *Home Rule for Scotland and Imperial Federation*, Scottish Home Rule Association, Edinburgh, p.i

[8] Constitution and Rules of the Scottish Home Rule Association, National Library of Scotland, Mf sp.102 (4)

[9] Resolution on Aims and Objects carried at the 1892 Annual General Meeting of the Scottish Home Rule Association. See the *Scotsman*, 4 June 1892, p.9

[10] John Ferguson addressing the 1892 Annual General Meeting of the Scottish Home Rule Association. See the *Scotsman*, 4 June 1892, p.9

[11] *Scotsman*, 4 June 1892, p.9

[12] James Mitchell, *Strategies for Self-Government*, 1996

[13] *Ibid*, p.73

[14] Until 1918 it was not possible to join the Labour Party as an individual. 'Membership' was confined to those who belonged to the trade unions and socialist societies affiliated to the Labour Party. The most significant society was the Independent Labour Party founded in 1893. After 1919, the ILP retained its own organisational structures and journal. Increasingly it became the left-wing of the Labour Party, and in Scotland it was the champion of the home rule tradition. In 1932 differences over Parliamentary Labour Party discipline, the economy, and the international situation led to the ILP disaffiliating from the Labour Party. In the 1935 general election the ILP, standing against the Labour Party, won four seats in Glasgow.

[15] *Scottish Home Rule, Newsletter of the Scottish Home Rule Association*, Vol. 9, No.11, September 1929. Please note that William Gallagher of the SCWS should not be confused with the Communist MP Willie Gallacher.

[16] See William Knox (ed.) *Scottish Labour Leaders 1918-1939: A Biographical Dictionary*, Mainstream, Edinburgh, 1984, pp.217-220

[17] Report of the 1919 Scottish Advisory Council of the Labour Party

[18] *Scottish Home Rule*, Vol.3, No.2, August 1922

[19] *Scottish Home Rule*, Vol.3, No.4, October 1922

[20] Scottish Home Rule Association, The Basis of the Association as amended at the Annual General Meeting held on 21 April 1923

[21] *Scottish Home Rule*, Vol.4, No.10, April 1924

[22] *Scottish Home Rule*, Vol.4, No.12, June 1924

[23] For an account of the debate see *Forward*, Vol.19, No.28, 17 May 1924, p.1

[24] Russell Galbraith, *Without Quarter: A Biography of Tom Johnston*, Mainstream, Edinburgh, 1995

[25] Jack Brand, *National Movement in Scotland*, 1978, p.178

[26] *Scottish Home Rule*, Vol.6, No.6, December 1925

[27] The debates were held on 13 May 1927 and 27 March 1928

[28] *Scottish Home Rule*, Vol.9, No.11, September 1929

[29] In 1934 the National Party of Scotland merged with the Scottish Party to form the Scottish National Party.

[30] Page Arnott, *The Miners: A History of the Miners' Federation of Great Britain 1889-1910*, George Allen and Unwin, London, 1949, p.132

[31] For a succinct biography of Cunninghame Graham, see L.G. Wickham Legg (ed.), *The Dictionary of National Biography 1931-1940*, 1949, pp. 354-356

[32] Figures listed in *Scottish Home Rule*, Vol.9, no.11, September 1929

[33] Scottish Co-operators of the 1920s prided themselves as more politically engaged than the movement elsewhere. They jealously guarded the right to negotiate staff wages and conditions at a Scottish level, and resisted attempts to absorb them in the British-wide negotiating structure.

[34] *Dalkeith Advertiser*, 17 January 1929

[35] *Ibid*, 24 Janaury 1929

[36] See John MacCormick, *The Flag In The Wind*, Gollancz, 1955

[37] Michael Keating and David Bleiman, *Labour and Scottish Nationalism*, Macmillan, London, 1979, pp.143-146

[38] Results quoted in the Scottish Convention pamphlet, *Questions We Are Asked?*, 1946

[39] Scottish Convention, 'Scottish National Assembly: Report of Proceedings, March 1947', 1948

[40] *Ibid*

[41] John Gollan, *Scottish Prospect: An Economic, Administrative and Social Survey*, Communist Party of Great Britain, 1948

[42] *Scotsman*, Monday 24 March 1947, p.6

[43] Scottish Convention, 'Scottish National Assembly: Report of Proceedings, March 1947', 1948

[44] John MacCormick, *The Flag in the Wind*, 1955, pp.12-13

[45] *Ibid*, pp.120-121

[46] *Ibid*, p.110

[47] *Scotsman*, 22 March, 1948, p.3

[48] Scottish Covenant Association, *Blue Print for Scotland: Practical Proposals for Scottish Self-Government*

[49] *Scotsman*, 31 October 1949, p.5

[50] Scottish Convention membership figures given in James Mitchell, *Strategies for Self-Government*, p.85

[51] The Committee on Scottish Financial Trade Statistics, chaired by Aberdeenshire-born Lord Catto, a former Governor of The Bank of England, was established in the summer of 1950. It was charged with calculating the total revenue derived from Scotland, and total government expenditure in Scotland. It was also asked to calculate Scottish imports and exports to establish Scotland's balance of payments with the rest of the United Kingdom and the wider world. When it reported to a Tory Secretary of State for Scotland in July 1952, it concluded there was 'no practicable method' for calculating Scottish imports and exports, and that only a rough estimation of Scottish revenues and Scottish share of public expenditure could be formed.

[52] Scottish Covenant Association, *The Covenant, Yesterday, Today, Tomorrow*, 1951

[53] Reported in the *Scotsman*, Monday 25 June 1951, p.1

[54] For an account of Labour's response to the SNP breakthrough see Robert McLean, *Labour and Scottish Home Rule*, Part II, *Scottish Labour Action*, Whitburn, 1990, pp.15-26

[55] For an account of the battle to legislate for a Scottish Assembly, see McLean, *Labour and Scottish Home Rule*, Part II, *Scottish Labour Action*, Whitburn, 1990, pp.26-31

CHAPTER 2

Nurturing the Flame

The establishment of the Campaign for a Scottish Assembly

The Referendum

AS A CONCESSION TO those in Labour's ranks who remained opposed to home rule, the Government declared in December 1976 that its Scottish Assembly proposals would be subject to a referendum in Scotland, despite the fact that there had been no suggestion of a referendum in Labour's October 1974 general election manifesto. Mindful that Labour had settled its differences over Europe by promising a referendum, a plebiscite on Scottish and Welsh devolution would allow anti-devolutionists in the Parliamentary Labour Party to continue to support the Government while reserving their position in the forthcoming referendum campaign.

Another instance of Labour's internal difficulties surfaced on 15 January 1979 when George Cunningham, an ex-patriate Scot representing a London constituency, moved an amendment to the effect that 40% of the registered Scottish electorate would have to support the Assembly in the referendum in order for it to be carried. The Government opposed the amendment, as did the Nationalists and the Liberals, but it was carried by an alliance of Tories and Labour anti-devolutionsists.[1]

The 40% rule, as it was known, was a democratic outrage. Given the average Scottish turnout in general elections, the Assembly would have to win the support of more than 60% of those turning out to vote. It was in reality a 'two-thirds' rule.[2] It was a hurdle that no United Kingdom government had ever cleared in a general election. It was an amendment designed to wreck the Assembly proposal. It was supported by five Scottish Labour MPs: Robin Cook, Tam Dalyell, Bob Hughes, Willie Hamilton and Peter Doig.[3] It was a measure which ultimately wrecked a Labour Government.

Yes and No

The March 1979 Devolution Referendum differed from the 1975 European vote in a number of important respects. There was no free circulation of information nor any state funding for the Yes and No umbrella campaigns. These omissions were driven by the Labour Party, rather than the Labour Government.[4] The thinking behind these decisions was revealed by Helen Liddell, then General Secretary of the Labour Party in Scotland. She told the press launch of the official Labour Movement Yes Campaign that, the STUC and the Co-operative Party aside, the Labour Party would not 'soil its hands' working with other parties for a Yes vote.[5]

On the national stage, and at its grassroots, Labour faced a major rebellion in the form of the Labour Vote No Campaign. The activities of Tam Dalyell, Brian Wilson, Robin Cook, Adam Ingram and Eric Milligan created confusion among Labour supporters as to the real Labour position, and mobilised powerful vested interests, particularly in the recently created regional tier of local government, against devolution.

Yes for Scotland

The main attempt to build a co-ordinated cross-party campaign for an Assembly was Yes For Scotland, which, while greatly under-resourced, attempted to involve pro-devolutionists from all political parties. It was formed only a matter of weeks before the referendum, in January 1979. It was chaired by Lord Kilbrandon, who had chaired the Royal Commission on the Constitution, and its vice chairs were the SNP's Margo MacDonald and Jim Sillars, leader of the short-lived Scottish Labour Party, which had broken away from the Labour Party in 1975.[6]

Writing in 1980, current Chancellor, Gordon Brown, criticised Yes for Scotland for failing to involve leading Labour and Conservative politicians and allowing itself to become dominated by the Nationalists and Sillars.[7] This criticism is neither accurate nor fair. A full year before Yes for Scotland was formed, the Executive of the Scottish Council of the Labour Party, of which Brown was a member, voted against participation in any cross-party campaign. Despite this prohibition, the National Committee of Yes for Scotland included Alex Kitson, Sir Simpson Stevenson and Professor Nigel Grant, leading figures in the trades unions, Labour local government and Labour academia.[8] The Communist Party also supported Yes for Scotland, providing another link to sections of the Labour movement. At its public launch on 4 January 1979, the Yes for Scotland platform included the late Brian Meek, then the leader of Edinburgh District Council. Leading Young Tories Paul Martin and Ian Hoy were also heavily involved in the Yes for Scotland organisation.[9] The leading SNP figures who participated in YFS, most particularly Margo Macdonald, did so as individuals. Officially, the Nationalists ran their own campaign.

The range of support obtained by Yes for Scotland later resurfaced in the Campaign for a Scottish Assembly/Parliament.

The No Men

Campaigns also proliferated on the No side, but their activities were co-ordinated through the Scotland Says No Campaign Committee. While Labour anti-devolutionists publicly distanced themselves from the Tory/business backed campaign, several senior Labour figures openly associated with it. One observer of the referendum campaign maintains that Labour Vote No was briefed by Scotland Says No.[10] Beyond doubt, Robin Cook and Tam Dalyell agreed to join Teddy Taylor and Ian Sproat as Honorary Presidents of the Student Campaign Against Devolution, a particularly noxious campaign organised by Aberdeen University student Peter Young, who later resurfaced as a leading light in the Adam Smith Institute.[11]

The Result and some reasons why

It should never be forgotten that the Yes campaigners won the referendum with 51.6%. But there is no denying that the slump, from a consistent 75% poll rating, was disappointing. Why? The best study of the Scottish Referendum of 1 March 1979 remains McCartney, Bochel and Denver, *The Referendum Experience*, and it is essential reading for students of Scottish home rule. Writing ten years later in *Radical Scotland*, Cairns Craig described the circumstances that forced Rip Mac Winkle into hibernation in 1979:

> 'Tormented by the West Lothian Question, bemused by the Referendum result, appalled by the Nationalists who wouldn't support a feeble Assembly, and by the Tories who thought that Sir Alex (Douglas Home) would give them a better one, and by the Labourites who didn't want their own Assembly – just in case it succeeded – Rick Mac Winkle took to the hills in 1979 and went to sleep.'[12]

John Kerr, then Scottish correspondent of the *Guardian*, warned before the referendum that somewhere along the road from 1974-1978, the Scottish people had 'talked themselves out' of the issue and no longer had the power of will to see it through.[13]

For me, one of the most surprising aspects of the referendum result was the No vote recorded in parts of the country which had elected Nationalist MPs in 1974: Highland, Grampian and Dumfries and Galloway. At the time of the referendum I was a sabbatical officer with the Students' Representative Council at the University of Aberdeen. During the campaign I worked with the Yes for Scotland Students Society on the campus, with Yes for Scotland and the Labour Movement Yes Campaign in the city. With the latter we made it a priority to leaflet the strongly Labour areas. I knew people who had been campaigning in Aberdeenshire, and along the Moray Firth, and they recounted the concern they had encountered at the prospect of a central-belt dominated Assembly which would ignore the concerns of rural Scotland. This was one of the reasons given by the Kilbrandon Commission for recommending the introduction of proportional representation for elections to a Scottish Assembly or Parliament. Despite the efforts of John P. Mackintosh, the Labour Party and Government refused to consider it. Earlier in the 1970s the joke did the rounds that a Scottish legislature would be dominated by 'Edinburgh lawyers and Glasgow Councillors'. Suddenly it wasn't that funny anymore.

Ray Perman, who covered Scotland for the *Financial Times* in 1979, concluded that:

> 'the Yes side failed to win a sufficient majority in the referendum because it was hopelessly divided and its arguments and efforts were often contradictory.'[14]

It was an analysis shared by those who went on to found the CSA.

The Fall of the Callaghan Government

The life of the Labour Government depended on establishing the Scottish Assembly. Failure to do so would result in the Nationalists and Liberals deserting the minority Callaghan government, opening it to the danger of a vote of no confidence. Following the failure of the referendum on 1 March came a rapid series of events. On 28 March, Tory leader Margaret Thatcher tabled her motion of no confidence. Despite some vintage rhetorical flourishes from Michael Foot, and avuncular gravitas from Callaghan, defeat in the debate was followed by defeat in the subsequent general election held on 3 May 1979. The Thatcher Era had begun.

The Nadir

With the implacably unreformed Unionist Margaret Thatcher in firm control at Westminster, the Scottish home rule question, which had dominated political debate in Scotland since 1967, and the Westminster agenda since 1974, seemed dead and buried. Tories who had flirted with the home rule cause either conformed or retired. Thatcher's radical right administration revived a Labour Left which believed that Labour had not been rejected because of its policies, but because its policies had never been implemented by the Wilson and Callaghan governments. Under the pressure of economic difficulties, the Labour government had drifted further and further from the Labour Party and opened the door to an ideology which rejected the principles on which the welfare state was founded.[15]

In the early years of the 1980s Labour was focussed on internal matters, procedures for selecting the Party Leader, and parliamentary candidates. Many in the party were more interested in devolving power within its own structures than the state. In the 1983 general election the Party had to fight to retain its position as the major opposition party as the alliance between the Liberal Party and the breakaway Social Democratic Party came close to out-polling Labour. While the Liberals remained loyal to their federalist policy, the prospect of 'preparing for power' at Westminster fixed their attention on the United Kingdom dimension.

The result of the 1979 Referendum, and the loss of nine of their eleven seats in the subsequent general election, deflated the Scottish National Party. It had been diverted by friction and factionalism over strategy. Where should the Party position itself on the Left/Right spectrum? How should it respond to future home rule measures which fell short of its goal of independence?

First Stirrings

Amid the gloom and recrimination, there were individuals prepared to carry on with a pro-home rule campaign, and, mindful of the referendum experience, to do so on the all-party/non-party basis that had distinguished earlier campaigns. Among the first to take an initiative was Jack Brand, a lecturer in politics at the University of Strathclyde. A member of the Scottish National Party, Brand's support for home rule was based on economic and democratic grounds, and the belief that responsibility for our own affairs would build more confident society.[16] The memories of those involved differ on when and where the forerunners of what became the Campaign for a Scottish Assembly first gathered. Isobel Lindsay recalls a meeting held a 'few months' after the referendum, in Community House in Glasgow's Clyde Street, at which a decision in principle was taken to launch a new campaign group.[17] Others who were involved recall that decisive meeting taking place in the autumn of 1979.[18] The thirty or so people present agreed to launch the new campaign on 1 March

1980, the first anniversary of the referendum, and continued to meet regularly in the interim to lay the political groundwork and organise the logistics.

So who were the individuals who forged ahead with the formation of the CSA? Jack Brand took the chair as interim convener while the jobs of interim secretary and interim treasurer were taken on by Duncan Thoms and Alan Wylie respectively. Thoms was a member of the Workers' Party of Scotland, a tiny Maoist sect which was best known for the criminal activity involving one of its members, and the charisma of its dominant figure, Spanish Civil War veteran Tom Murray. Wylie was a Glasgow lawyer and a Liberal.[19] Others included: Hugh Miller, at that time representing the John MacLean Society, former Labour councillor Jim Boyack, Doug Bain, brother of fiddle maestro Ally and Glasgow District Secretary of the Communist Party of Great Britain, academic and SNP activist, Isobel Lindsay, whose involvement with the Campaign for Nuclear Disarmament ensured she was a weel-kent face on the Scottish left, Nigel Grant, Professor of Education at the University of Glasgow, Dennis Canavan, Member of Parliament for West Stirlingshire, and Joe Farrell, a senior figure in Jim Sillars' breakaway Scottish Labour Party.[20]

Then there was Jim Sillars and George Foulkes. Sillars was a product of Labour's Ayrshire machine, who had broken with the Party over home rule in 1975, the very point at which Labour was taking the issue seriously for the first time in 20 years. Foulkes had been a colleague of Jim Boyack's on Edinburgh Co-operation and shared his enthusiasm for home rule. Foulkes had risen to the chair of Edinburgh's Education Committee under Jack Kane's groundbreaking Labour administration. In the 1979 general election, Foulkes defeated the incumbent Sillars in South Ayrshire, and Isobel Lindsay recalls the frosty atmosphere between them at early planning meetings.[21]

Cheering on from the sidelines were the influential Jimmy Milne, the Communist General Secretary of the STUC and Hugh Wyper, Communist Regional Secretary of the Transport and General Workers' Union.[22] The support of the Communist Party partly explains the early and consistent backing received from the National Union of Mineworkers in Scotland.

There was some uncertainty as to when the new campaign should go public. Hugh Miller recalls that his John MacLean Society colleague, Maurice Blythman, sought to push matters on by moving a resolution that the Campaign should be formed on 1 March 1980. Jack Brand responded that the meeting was informal and that there were no standing orders covering resolutions. Blythman quipped that he wanted to move a 'proto motion'. His point was not lost on those present and the meeting agreed to go ahead with the launch.[23]

The next few months were spent rallying support for the official launch on Saturday 1 March 1980. Hugh Miller was quick off the mark. Using his Yes for Scotland and political party networks he contacted sympathisers in the Edinburgh area, and an initial informal gathering of supporters was held in the Workers' Educational Association premises in Riddels Court, off the Lawnmarket. The meeting agreed to call a second, wider meeting which took place on 9 February 1980.[24] One of the striking features of the Campaign for a Scottish Assembly/Parliament throughout its history was the strength of its Edinburgh Branch. Those early foundations may help explain why.

Launching the Campaign for a Scottish Assembly

The public launch of the Campaign for a Scottish Assembly was held in Edinburgh on Saturday 1 March 1980, the first anniversary of the ill-fated devolution referendum, and was attended by an estimated 400 people. Contrary to the details given in some available secondary sources, the meeting took place in the premises of Edinburgh & District Trades Council in Edinburgh's Picardy Place.[25]

In the run up to the launch, the Scottish press, convinced that home rule was dead for a generation, paid more attention to Mark Thatcher's racing sponsorship from 'girlie club king', Paul Raymond, and to the late Willie Ormond's attempts to entice the errant, but brilliant, George Best to Easter Road. The press verdict on the Campaign's prospects was summed up by Chris Baur' sketch of the 'scattered and demoralised' forces of home rule 'creeping back down the hills', while a *Glasgow Herald* cartoon depicted a tentative and bashful lion attempting to revive a tartan-clad beauty named 'Assembly'.[26]

The mood at the launch was altogether more upbeat. It was chaired by Jack Brand, and among those who spoke were: George Foulkes, Ray Michie, Vice Chair of the Scottish Liberals, John Home-Robertson MP, Neil MacCormick, son of the Covenant movement leader, Margo MacDonald, Labour academics Bernard Crick and Nigel Grant, and Miners' leader George Bolton. Una MacLean Mackintosh informed the assembled that her late husband, John Mackintosh, MP and political scientist, expressed his regret at the outcome of the referendum result from his death bed. There was a warm welcome for Conservative Helen Miller, and a few groans from those who regarded Dennis Canavan's attacks on the Tories as devisive.[27]

The founding declaration carried by the meeting contained, as its 'second immediate objective', the creation of:

'A National Convention representative of Scottish life and society to consider detailed proposals for the constitution and powers of a Scottish Assembly.'[28]

Pre-figuring the key role that she would play ten years later in the Scottish Constitutional Convention, Isobel Lindsay told the meeting that the job of such a convention would be to:

'work out what the Scots really wanted.'

As a SNP member she was ready to concede that what they wanted was not independence, but she was prepared to work out the maximum possible consensus.[29]

The founding declaration demonstrated that the concept of a Constitutional Convention was as central to the CSA as the Scottish National Convention and the Scottish National Assembly had been to the second Scottish Home Rule Association and the Covenant movement.

The launch rally concluded by confirming the three interim office bearers: Brand, Thoms and Wylie. By a process of nomination and self-nomination a further thirty people were appointed to the first CSA National Committee, which would serve until an inaugural general

meeting later in the year. They included several of the people mentioned already: Jim Boyack, Hugh Miller, Una MacLean Mackintosh
and Joe Farrell. Others included: Colin Boyd, Edinburgh lawyer, a
member of Sillars' Scottish Labour Party and now Lord Advocate in
a Scottish government, The Very Reverend David Steel, former
Moderator of the Church of Scotland, and Greg McCarra. Of the 39
members of the first CSA National Committee, 7 were associated with
Labour, 7 with the SNP and 4 with the Liberal Party.[30]

During the following week, on 6 March 1980, thirty one Glasgow
supporters gathered in the Trade Union Centre in Carlton Place, on
the south side of the Clyde, to form an interim Glasgow Committee
of the Campaign for a Scottish Assembly. The Communist Party's Doug
Bain was elected as the Acting Convener, SNP activist Greg McCarra
was elected as Secretary and Conservative Helen Miller was elected as
Treasurer. The job of the interim officers was to build for an inaugural meeting on 18 May 1980 at which the Glasgow Branch of the
CSA would be constituted. Doug Bain and Greg McCarra continued
as the principal officers until May 1981 when they were replaced by
Eric Canning (Convener) and Jim Whitson (Secretary), a partner-
ship which was to serve the Glasgow Branch of the CSA during the
early years of its existence.[31]

While the Scotsman's Chris Baur dismissed the ranks of the CSA for
lacking 'generals', and dismissed the convention proposal as 'fanciful',
he himself unearthed a 'general' prepared to argue for a convention. In
his coverage of the CSA launch, Baur interviewed STUC General
Secretary, Jimmy Milne, who described the Scotland Act as:

'the creature of Westminster politicians who were only concerned with slinging together something that could get through
parliament.'

But how, asked Baur, could the implacably Unionist majority be
compelled to address fresh demands for devolution? Milne replied:

'By making the Mark II Bill a creature of a representative
Scottish Convention.'[32]

It was an early and succinct summation of the strategy the CSA would pursue over the next 20 years.

Initial Reactions

Within weeks of the launch of the CSA, the Scottish Liberals met in conference and expressed full support for the Campaign.[33] From the outset, Labour in Scotland maintained an arms-length approach towards the CSA. George Foulkes, who had been involved in planning the launch of the CSA, established the Labour Campaign for a Scottish Assembly at Labour's Scottish Conference later in March 1980. Foulkes was reported to have warned the CSA about becoming dominated by the SNP.[34] This led the *Scotsman* to conclude in June 1980 that:

> 'the Labour Party hierarchy have been conspicuous by their lack of support for the all party grouping.'[35]

The SNP response was in some ways similar to that of the Labour Party. While Labour was wary of being compromised by the SNP within an all-party campaign, many in the SNP had concerns about supporting campaigns whose goal fell short of independence. This concern aside, leading SNP figures appeared on early CSA platforms, and in November 1980, SNP President Billy Wolfe declared he would work with any individual or group that was 'genuine' about securing some form of home rule. Jack Brand responded quickly, through the pages of the *Glasgow Herald*, arguing that the CSA was such an organisation.[36]

The CSA pioneers had grounds for believing that their advocacy of a constitutional convention would be attractive to elements in the SNP. When Harold Wilson first attempted to legislate for devolution, the Scotland and Wales Bill was 'talked' out in February 1977. Donald Bain, the Party's influential Research Officer floated the idea of an elected assembly which would debate and agree its own powers and then negotiate with Westminster on that basis. In the month that the CSA was launched, March 1980, SNP leader Gordon Wilson presented a Bill to create a constitutional convention. He continued to promote the idea, and in 1984 it became SNP policy.[37] Despite Wilson's support for some kind of convention, his hostility to co-operating across party boundaries prevented the SNP leader and the CSA from working towards the common goal of a convention.

In the early years of its existence in particular, the CSA tried to involve pro-devolution Conservatives in the campaign. Brian Meek, Paul Martin, John Young and the East Lothian District Council Conservative Group were all courted by the CSA at one time or another. In an attempt to save the already mentioned Scotland and Wales Bill, Francis Pym, then Tory spokesman on constitutional matters, proposed an all-party conference to discuss home rule for Scotland and Wales. It was enough to persuade the Liberals to vote against a guillotine designed to save the legislation. Following the Tory victory in 1979, Pym, and other Tories known to support devolution, yielded to unreformed Unionist orthodoxy.[38]

An early opportunity for the CSA to engage with Scotland's political parties occurred in June 1980 when the Glasgow Branch of the CSA decided to intervene in the Glasgow Central by election. With the financial and political support of the National Committee, the Glasgow Branch distributed an A5 flyer in the constituency. One side promoted the CSA while the flip-side listed the responses of each of the candidates on where they stood in relation to home rule.

Labour's Bob McTaggart pledged support for the 1978 proposals while the Tories' Anna McCurley pronounced devolution dead. The Ecology Party candidate and the 'Young Liberal' candidate advocated a federal approach while the SNP's Gill Paterson called for independence.[39]

In an attempt to build support across the political spectrum, representatives of the CSA trooped from Perth, to Dunoon, to Inverness, to Aberdeen, and other favouite conference venues, to carry the debate to the conferences of Scotland's political parties and institutions.

The first ever CSA fringe meeting took place at the STUC Congress in Perth on 23 April 1980. The venue was the Isle of Skye Hotel. The platform included Deputy General Secretary, John Henry, and the miners' George Bolton. They were joined by Jim Ross. Jim had been a senior civil servant at the Scottish Office and had responsibility for the Wilson/Callaghan devolution plans. Jim's encyclopaedic knowledge of the subject and his commanding presentation made him one of the CSA's 'big hitters', who would play a vital role in the years ahead. The fringe meeting was attended by some twenty people. A modest audience perhaps, but the start of a key relationship between the STUC and the CSA.[40]

The most important campaigning initiative of the CSA's first summer was The Festival of the People organised on Edinburgh's Calton Hill on Saturday 28 June 1980 by the Edinburgh Branch of the Campaign.

The Festival of the People

From the launch of the CSA, Edinburgh provided the largest pool of activists. For several years in the history of the Campaign, the Edinburgh Branch included more than 50% of the national membership. Edinburgh was the first branch to be inaugurated, and from its earliest days it undertook ambitious projects. During the CSA's first summer it was the Edinburgh Branch that took on responsibility for the Campaign's first large-scale public event, The Festival of the People, held on Calton Hill on Saturday 28 June 1980. The idea for the event was to be found in the fetes and fiestas associated with the democratic socialist and euro-communist parties of Western Europe, where political speeches took their place alongside food, theatre, music and sport.[41] The organisers, which included Hugh Miller and Colin Boyd, attempted to emulate the Continental flavour, by including decorated floats, drama and music in promoting the home rule cause.

At the end of the day The Festival was relatively successful. There was one decorated float and an estimated turnout of 500 people. The 7:84 Theatre Company performed a thirty minute excerpt from their current production, *Joe's Drum*, and the event ended with a ceilidh in the Zetland Halls in Pilrig Street. Another element of the day was the inaugural Seven Hills Race.[42] This was organised by Edinburgh Branch member Alan Lawson and provided a sporting component to the Festival. It proved so popular that it took on a life of its own and still takes place twenty years on.[43] The Festival bequeathed another legacy. Staging the event on Calton Hill associated the Campaign with the old Royal High School building, which was the intended venue for Labour's proposed Scottish Assembly. Standing empty, with the exception of security staff and guard dogs, it visualised the denial of democracy to the Scottish people. With picture opportunities in mind, the Edinburgh campaigners fashioned a giant key to open the gates locked against home rule. In the years that followed the key did the rounds of CSA events.[44]

As far as speakers at The Festival were concerned, John Henry and George Bolton reprised their roles at the CSA fringe meeting at the STUC Congress back in April. They were joined on the platform by Jim Sillars, Hugh Miller and CSA National Chairman Jack Brand. Henry, Miller and Sillars all referred to the symbolism of Calton Hill while Brand stressed the single issue nature of the CSA.[45]

While the Edinburgh Branch was setting the pace in local organisation, work was underway elsewhere to establish other branches. The minutes of the National Committee report contacts made in East Lothian, Greenock, Inverness, Dunbartonshire, Perth, Ayr and Dundee, while a working conference was held in Glasgow on 18 May 1980. The pattern of branch activity can be explained by the presence in each area of activists who were already networked with the national organisation. Given Glasgow's political traditions, the failure to sustain a branch on the same scale as Edinburgh was an ongoing concern.

An important task for the interim National Committee was to organise a conference which would adopt a constitution for the CSA. The meeting took place in the University of Strathclyde on Saturday 29 November 1980. In addition to adopting a constitution, the conference also discussed electoral systems for a Scottish Assembly, the financing of the Assembly and the economic powers that should be devolved, three issues which would continue to dominate the home rule debate until the late 1990s.[46]

The Edinburgh Festival of the People convinced the Glasgow Branch of the CSA to follow the conference on 29 November with a St Andrew's Day Festival of the People, held in the McLellan Galleries on Sunday 30 November. The initial publicity boasted an impressive line up. Phil Mcall would compere events in the main hall programme, which included Jazz music, Russell Hunter, Alastair McDonald and a 'brains trust' of political commentators chaired by Bill Tenant. There would be stalls galore and Hamish Henderson would read poetry in the east room.[47] Those involved with the event remember it as 'just credible'. The total turnout throughout the Sunday afternoon was 200, just half of the 500 expected. There were criticisms of the design and distribution of the publicity for the event, but the event also suffered from billed participants failing to appear.[48]

The first national leaflet produced by the CSA, in the spring of 1981, called for the convening of a National Convention 'of all shades of Scottish opinion'.[49] It soon became clear to even the most optimistic that the convening of a credible representative convention was a long way off. The National Committee therefore agreed to call its own CSA National Convention and throw it open to anyone interested in discussing the theme of the event.

The First CSA National Convention

Invitations to the first CSA National Convention were distributed by Duncan Thoms as Secretary.[50] It was held in the Assembly Rooms, in Edinburgh's George Street, on 28 March 1981. The morning session was devoted to the political, economic and cultural case for home rule, while the afternoon was a discussion of the powers of an Assembly, and a strategy as to how that Assembly could be realised.[51] It appears that the National Committee envisaged the morning session as a 'girning session' which would allow people to voice their frustrations before dealing with the more substantive afternoon agenda.[52]

Press coverage of the first CSA National Convention concentrated on a paper suggesting increased economic powers for a Scottish Assembly, beyond those listed in the Scotland Act, e.g. control of the levers of economic planning, the Scottish Development Agency and the Highland and Islands Development Board, and a proposed funding formula based on guaranteed percentage take from selected taxes, as well as a needs assessment.[53]

Commentators present at the first CSA National Convention noted a perceived predominance of SNP activists, and while there was some press interest prior to the event, there was little coverage of the outcomes. This may have been due to the unfortunate scheduling that allowed the event to clash with the Scottish Liberal Conference. The 1981 Liberal Conference in Galashiels was very significant as it came at the end of the week in which the Social Democratic Party had been formed. Robert McLellan, the only Scottish Labour MP to breakaway, represented the SDP at Galashiels, and UK Liberal Leader, David Steel, used the occasion to express his preference for a 'full alliance' and not a tepid non-aggression pact between the two parties.[54]

The Scottish Question, however, featured large in the early courtship of the star-crossed allies. The list of Labour policies, which the breakaway Social Democrats cited as their reasons for leaving, included devolution for Scotland and Wales. Realising that this represented a potential turn-off to the Liberal keepers of the home rule tradition, the backpeddling Social Democrats were at pains to explain that they were in favour of decentralisation but opposed Labour's unilateral, or 'lopsided' policy, which they intended to replace with a British-wide regional government scheme.[55] Steel made it clear at Galashiels that Scotland could not wait for home rule all round, but should act as pace-setter for constitutional reform.[56] Donald Gorrie warned that the establishment of a Scottish Assembly was non-negotiable while Menzies Campbell added electoral reform to the list.[57]

Earlier, while briefing the press ahead of the forthcoming CSA National Convention, Jack Brand expressed his belief that a clear majority of CSA activists supported an Assembly with an 'economic remit and a proportional method of election.'[58]

Jack Brand

In his study of Scottish home rule initiatives, Professor James Michell, who has worked with Brand, suggests that the CSA's first convener was opposed to the campaign over-concerning itself with a new devolution settlement. As far as Brand was concerned, the Labour Party was key. It was the serious contender for power at Westminster and most likely to deliver constitutional change. Brand appreciated the need to revisit those elements of the Scotland Act that had proved to be hostages to fortune during the referendum campaign but opposed fundamental revisions that might frighten Labour off.[59]

Mitchell has cited an article by Brand in the Left/Nationalist magazine, *Cran Tara*, in the spring of 1981 as a statement of the latter's cautious approach.[60] Brand's concern about the CSA's position as a single issue campaign may have been influenced by the activities of the Edinburgh Branch.

A Small Victory

In June of 1981, Colin Boyd, by then Chair of the Edinburgh Branch, wrote to the Mergers and Monopolies Commission calling on it to travel to Scotland to take evidence on the proposed merger of the Royal Bank of Scotland with Standard and Charter.[61] Boyd was expressing the fear of the Branch, and many other Scots, that the merger threatened to remove decision making in a major Scottish financial institution from Scotland. The Edinburgh CSA invited the Royal Bank to put its view, but having heard its general manager and head economist, the Branch was unconvinced, and agreed to make a submision to the Commission opposing the merger.[62]

Billie Fraser, at that point Secretary of the Edinburgh CSA, recalls Brand visiting the Branch and gently forwarding the view that institutional mergers were outwith the aims and objects of the CSA. By the end of the evening, however, the National Chairman agreed to add the weight of the Campaign as a whole to the Edinburgh Branch's submission.[63]

Ultimately, the Edinburgh initiative was successful on two counts. The Monopolies and Mergers Commission travelled north for the first time and took evidence in Scotland during the first week in September 1981.[64] In early January 1982 the Commission ruled against the merger. In their report the Commissioners stated:

'opposition to control of any major English or Scottish clearing bank passing overseas into the hands of those not fully committed to the United Kingdom interest carried a good deal of weight.'[65]

A New Blue Print

Following the first CSA National Convention in March 1981 there was a job to be done in distilling the various points raised, and defining the areas of disagreement over a new Assembly package. The job was given to Colin Boyd. By October 1981 Colin had completed his task. The result was the pamphlet *Blue Print*. Taking its name from the Covenant movement's home rule plan, *Blue Print* was launched at a CSA press conference in late October. An initial 5,000 copies of *Blue Print* were widely circulated to promote discussion in the run up to the second CSA National Convention scheduled for April 1982.[66]

Blue Print recorded the degree of agreement over the areas to be devolved and those to be retained at Westminster. It represented a move forward from the Assembly on offer in 1979, and the range of powers earmarked for Edinburgh are very similar to those now controlled by the Scottish Parliament, although broadcasting was listed in the devolved column.[67]

Blue Print was less sure when it came to financing the Assembly. The first CSA National Convention expressed a preference for a financing package structured to minimise potential interference from Westminster, and for oil revenues to be included. *Blue Print* sought to discipline future discussion by defining the three alternative models. They were:

- A Block Grant as per the 1979 Scotland Act

- The allocation of a guaranteed percentage of UK taxes to the Assembly

- Full revenue-raising powers with the Assembly paying a reverse block grant to Westminster for UK services.

With regard to the structure of the Assembly, *Blue Print* envisaged a 100-200 member legislature with an Executive of 10-12 members, including a prime minister. On the question of how the Assembly Members should be elected, *Blue Print* referred to the 'widespread support for a system of proportional representation' expressed at the first Campaign Convention, but left the precise system as a matter for future debate.[68] From the publication of *Blue Print* in October 1981, however, it was generally accepted that the CSA supported the principle of proportional representation.

During the 1979 referendum campaign, the Tories promised that meetings of the Scottish Grand Committee would take place in Scotland. The first meeting of the Scottish Grand Committee held north of the border took place on 15 February 1982. Jack Brand seized the opportunity to rubbish the notion that Grand Committee meetings in Edinburgh were any kind of serious alternative to legislative devolution. Brand called on all Scottish MPs to attend the CSA's second National Convention scheduled for 30 March 1982. Donald Dewar's response was interesting. He told the *Glasgow Herald* that he doubted if many Scottish Labour MPs would take up the invitation to attend the CSA event, and that Labour would work for devolution through the established party system, 'rather than through this pressure group.'[69]

The Second CSA National Convention, 20 March 1982

Dewar's cynicism aside, the second Campaign Convention was held in Edinburgh's Assembly Rooms, under the strapline 'Let Scotland Speak', and among those who did were John Pollock, General Secretary of the Educational Institute of Scotland and Chair of the STUC, and Russell Johnston MP, Leader of the Scottish Liberal Party. Both of them called for maximum unity in the drive to win an Assembly.[70] In its first edition, *Radical Scotland* reported that the Convention was attended by some 200 people. Those who expressed a party allegiance on their registration forms were equally divided between the SNP, Liberals and Labour.[71]

When it came to debating *Blue Print*, most of the document was enthusiastically endorsed. The one exception was the finance section. The nationalists present called for a reverse block grant, arguing that the struggle underway between Scottish local authorities and the Scottish Office illustrated how an Assembly, without fiscal autonomy, could be undermined by Westminster.[72]

Compromise was achieved around a proposal from Bill Speirs, then Assistant General Secretary of the STUC. Bill advocated that the three options outlined in *Blue Print* should be replaced by a single system in which the Assembly would be partly financed by a block grant, would have the right to supplement its revenues via a local income tax, and that a percentage of oil, tobacco and alcohol revenues should be paid directly to the Assembly. The Speirs proposal had its critics, who argued that the suggestion of Scots paying additional taxes for home rule was the Achilles Heel of Scottish devolution. At the conclusion of the debate, the Speirs alternative was adopted in principle with a remit to the CSA National Committee to refine it further.[73] That debate, at the second CSA National Convention in March 1982 put the question of fiscal autonomy at the heart of the issue.

Another significant point to emerge from the 1982 CSA National Convention was a declaration from the National Committee arguing that the membership of a future Constitutional Convention should be directly elected.[74]

In the run up to the National Convention in March 1982, there were a couple of significant changes in the membership of the National Committee. SNP member Greg McCarra took over the Secretary's role and Eric Canning, of the Communist Party, joined the Committee.[75]

Enter the Social Democrats

The launch and by election success of the Social Democrats prompted the demand for clarification on where this new political force stood on home rule, particularly as they cited Labour's proposed Scottish Assembly as one of their reasons for breaking with the party. An early opportunity to pose the question arose from the death of Glasgow's remaining Tory MP, Tam Galbraith, in early 1982. Immense media attention focussed on the Glasgow Hillhead when Roy Jenkins, former

Labour Cabinet member and one of the Gang of Four, emerged as the SDP candidate. The CSA brokered a well attended all-party hustings in Partick Burgh Halls. Labour's Dave Wiseman, Jenkins, the SNP's George Leslie and Ecologist Nicola Carslaw all participated, but Tory Gerry Malone declined.[76]

When pressed on home rule, Jenkins argued that he and his colleagues had opposed Labour's 'lop-sided proposals', and promised a major policy statement on decentralisation.[77]

Victorious in Hillhead, Jenkins delivered on his promise in July 1982, when the SDP called for thirteen regional assemblies, elected by proportional representation, as part of a package of constitutional reforms that included abolition of the Lords and the introduction of single-tier local government.[78] While the neatness of the SDP's policy gained plaudits for its symmetry, there were concerns within the CSA, not least among Liberals, that it smacked of utopianism, and failed to appreciate the different degrees of regional identity across the United Kingdom and the fact that Scotland could not wait for home rule all round. Positive engagement was the order of the day however and leading SDP figures were co-opted on to the CSA National Committee.

Thinking the Unthinkable

The initial impact of the SDP, and the jingoism surrounding the Falklands War, cast doubts over Labour's ability to form a government after the next general election, which was expected sometime in 1983. On 29 September 1982, George Galloway addressed the Edinburgh Branch of the CSA on the subject of Labour and Self-government.[79] A leading light on Labour's Scottish Executive, a darling of the Labour Left, and the Party's full-time organiser in Dundee, Galloway was one of the first senior Labour figures to think the unthinkable. How would Scotland react if Thatcher won again in England?[80]

Galloway was not alone. During the summer of 1982 the Scottish media regularly reported on unnamed Scottish MPs who seemed ready to jump on the independence bandwagon if Labour seemed stuck in perpetual opposition. *Sunday Standard* editor, Tom James, claimed that as many as fourteen Labour MPs were moving to that position, led by George Foulkes, John Home Robertson, John Maxton and David Marshall.[81]

The stirrings in Labour ranks, the SDP's decentralisation proposals and Gordon Wilson's call for a Constitutional Convention persuaded the Scottish media that home rule, which had seemed to be a dead duck in the spring of 1979, was rising up the political agenda in the summer of 1982.

To maintain pressure on opposition MPs, the CSA issued a questionnaire to all candidates, asking where they stood on home rule, and, in particular, would they support the calling of a Constitutional Convention if the Tories emerged triumphant from the next general election?[82]

Jim Boyack Takes the Chair

In the autumn of 1982, The Campaign for a Scottish Assembly responded to the crisis in the Scottish Steel industry by issuing what the *Glasgow Herald* described as, 'the most bitter attack yet on the Government,'[83]

The CSA National Committee statement issued on 8 September 1982 pledged the CSA to:

'help rally progressive democratic forces against this Government which in its essence and actions is anti-Scottish.'

It went on to:

'call upon moderate Conservatives for their support, even in an unofficial capacity, and urges the progressive forces in Scotland to press for urgently needed changes of policy.'

The predictable Conservative response was delivered by their Scottish Vice President, Alastair Smith, who charged the CSA National Committee with undermining its own position by 'adopting such a clearly partisan position.'[84] Smith may not have been the only one unhappy with the CSA statement. The statement was issued in the name of Jim

Boyack, the Campaign's Vice Chair. Within a matter of weeks, Jim succeeded Jack Brand as National Chairman of the CSA.

In the twenty years of its existence, the Campaign for a Scottish Assembly/Parliament underwent three major organisational reviews. In the early years an annual gathering of individual members and affiliated organisations elected a National Committee, which in turn elected a group of officers who acted as the Campaign's Executive. It was at a meeting of the National Committee on 11 December 1982 that Jim Boyack took over as the National Chairman of the Campaign for a Scottish Assembly, a post he was to hold until 1988. Among the other Executive members elected on that occasion were Vice Chairs Hugh Miller and Sir John Brotherstone. Hugh had a long pedigree on the nationalist left dating back to the 1960s, and had been centrally involved in the discussions that led to the establishment of the CSA. Along with Colin Boyd and others he was responsible for building the Edinburgh Branch. Sir John Brotherstone was a former Chief Medical Officer for Scotland and Professor of Community Medicine at the University of Edinburgh. Val Marshall succeeded Greg McCarra as Secretary and Charles Whyte from Perth became National Treasurer.[85]

Commenting on his decision to step down as Chair, Jack Brand told the media he was doing so to 'concentrate his efforts on studies of the political nature of the Assembly.'[86] Events suggest that he was not particularly comfortable with campaigns to prevent the Royal Bank merger and withering condemnations of general government economic and social policy. Brand wanted to stick pretty close to the 1978 Scotland Act, with the obvious anomalies rectified. The best chance of establishing an Assembly was the return of a Labour government, and the party would be more likely to champion a scheme with which it was broadly familiar. Others in the CSA clearly favoured a settlement far in advance of the 1978 proposal.

If Brand did harbour these concerns he did not dwell on them in his final report to the National Committee. In what added up to a political balance sheet, Brand identified the CSA's early successes as:

- establishing that all of Scotland's major political parties, with the obvious exception, supported home rule in principle

- the two Campaign Conventions called by the CSA had attracted the support of senior political figures

- effective campaigning around the Glasgow Hillhead by election which boded well for pressure group work at the forthcoming general election.

- the determination of the Campaign to hold politicians to the promise of early action on legislating for an Assembly.

When it came to listing disappointments, the departing Brand cited the indifference and hostility of English politicians to the notion of home rule, and he called on the CSA to open a cross-border dialogue.[87]

The circumstances of Brand's departure aside, his colleagues took to heart his comments about taking the Campaign south of the border, and on 15/16 February 1983, the first in a series of CSA Westminster lobbies took place. The CSA delegation consisted of Jim Boyack and Val Marshall. They met with North of England Labour MPs, including John Prescott, and the question of how an Assembly would be elected dominated much of their discussions with Scottish Labour MPs. The CSA pair also met with Roy Jenkins and Robert McLennan of the SDP and had informal discussions with Tories Alick Buchanan Smith and Malcolm Rifkind who promised their personal support for thought out constitutional reform. The SNP's Donald Stewart pledged not to stand in the way of meaningful devolution legislation.[88]

There was general agreement that, if the Campaign was to seriously tackle the challenges ahead, it must transform its resources.[89] In December 1982 the new Executive issued an appeal for £10,000 with the aim of renting an office with part-time staff cover. By early March 1983, the Executive could report that enough had been raised to open an office in the Saltire Society's Edinburgh headquarters.[90]

The Third CSA National Convention, 9 April 1983

The third CSA campaign Convention met in Edinburgh's Assembly Rooms on Saturday 9 April 1983. Organised around the theme 'Crisis in the Scottish Economy' the CSA was alert to the fact that it was being held in the final countdown to a general election. The SNP had decided against sending an official delegation, but there were many SNP members among the 350 people present. New Chairman, Jim Boyack opened the event with the kind of upbeat message that became his hallmark. George Foulkes reported that former Labour doubters had been won over by the impact of Tory policies on Scotland. A more cautious note was sounded by Professor Chris Harvie, who compared the turnout to the estimated 16,000 people gathered in Melrose for the annual seven-a-side rugby tournament.[91] A leading light among Labour-supporting, pro-devolution academia, Chris Harvie was a regular feature on CSA platforms in the 1980s. Quitting Labour for the SNP, Chris Harvie has written widely on Scottish history and politics and the developing European dimension. He is currently Professor of British and Irish studies at the University of Tubingen in Germany.

Perhaps the most significant outcome of the third Convention was the decision to reconvene within three months of the general election to review the political landscape.

The 1983 General Election: Outcomes and Implications

The general election of June 1983 confirmed diverging political cultures among the nations of the United Kingdom. The Conservatives were runaway winners in the UK as a whole, but in Scotland their 28.4% share of the vote confirmed the steady decline in Tory support in Scotland from the 50% high achieved in 1955.

On paper, the Liberals and Social Democrats appeared to be the main beneficiaries, with their Alliance winning 24% of the Scottish poll, compared with the 9% gained by the Liberals in 1979. Within the Alliance, however, there was deep disappointment that votes had failed to translate into seats, outwith the Liberals' traditional rural fiefdoms. Disappointment too at SNP headquarters where their vote declined to 11.7%, far removed from the 30.4% captured in the heady heights of October 1974.[92]

As the largest party in Scotland, Labour had a mandate of sorts, but its confidence had been knocked by the 31.5% polled in Scotland and, more so, by the 27.6% polled in England and Wales, just 1.4% ahead of the Liberal/SDP Alliance.

Constitutional Convention on the Agenda

It had been obvious to any candid observer of British politics that Mrs Thatcher was heading for a second election triumph in the spring of 1983. With the resolutely anti-home rule Thatcher back in power, what prospect for any movement on the Assembly question? In response, the officers of the CSA revisited the 'immediate aim' adopted by the founding conference. A representative Constitutional Convention, promoting a consensus plan for an Assembly scheme, could apply unprecedented pressure on the government.[93]

Accordingly, the first CSA initiative following the 1983 general election was not the promised recall Convention – that would happen later – but an Agenda Conference to which Scotland's political parties, the STUC and CBI, were invited to discuss: a) the implications of the general election and b) the CSA's proposal for a Constitutional Convention.[94] It took place in the North British Hotel in Edinburgh on Saturday 9 July. As expected, the Conservative Party and the CBI declined the invitation but there was real disappointment when the Labour Party followed suit. Credible delegations were sent by the Scottish Liberals, the SNP, the SDP, the Communist Party and the Ecologists. The STUC delegation included General Secretary, Jimmy Milne, his deputy John Henry and the Transport Workers' Hugh Wyper. The CSA delegation included Jim Boyack, Hugh Miller, Greg McCarra and Paul Scott. Labour MP Dennis Canavan attended in a personal capacity.[95]

On behalf of the CSA Greg McCarra introduced the Campaign's formative ideas on the membership of a Constitutional Convention, and a timetable leading to its convening. Jimmy Milne, Gordon Wilson and Russell Johnston all expressed concern at Labour's absence, and the view that progress on a Convention could not be made without the involvement of the largest pro-home rule party. Dennis Canavan stressed that the Convention proposal was not understood, never mind supported, by most people in the Labour Party, and that a massive debate would have to take place in its ranks if progress was to be made. Milne promised to bring what influence the STUC could to bear upon the Labour Party.[96]

The distance the Labour Party would have to travel if it was to participate in what would become known as the 'Inter Party Initiative' was demonstrated a few months later. Responding to a general CSA trawl for affiliations, Helen Liddell, the Party's Scottish General Secretary. wrote:

'it would not be appropriate for us to affiliate to the Campaign for a Scottish Assembly.'[97]

Liddell's reply was reminiscent of the 1919 decision of the Scottish Council of the Labour Party not to affiliate to the Scottish Home Rule Association. Liddell ruled that, under guidelines produced by Labour's National Executive in London, the Party in Scotland could not affiliate to the CSA. This ruling baffled many Scottish Labour Executive members, given that they were affiliated to a wide range of organisations. Liddell, however, did not rule out informal contacts which constituted the nature of the relationship between Labour and the CSA until 1989.

The question of Labour's position aside, the SDP's Peter Wilson insisted that proportional representation for an Assembly, and reform of local government, were preconditions for their involvement in a Convention. The insistence on PR was echoed by the Liberals and Ecologists. Responding for the CSA, Jim Boyack acknowledged the significance of fair elections to a future Scottish Assembly, but said massive debate would be required if Labour was to support that position.[98]

The Agenda Conference concluded with the issuing of a joint communique, which argued that cross party action was essential to achieve Scottish home rule, and that the Agenda Conference had been an important first step. It called on those reported missing to join in the ongoing discussion.[99]

The Re-Call CSA National Convention

As promised, the National Convention of the CSA was recalled within three months of the general election, on 17 September 1983 in the Mitchell Theatre in Glasgow, as an immediate follow on from the CSA's Annual General Meeting. The danger of the occasion dissolving into a 'greeting meeting' was avoided by the positive noises emerging from the Agenda Conference process. On behalf of the CSA officers, Greg McCarra reprised the thinking on the Constitutional Convention's composition and remit, and it was agreed that a dedicated workshop on the details should be held on 3 December at Saltire House in Edinburgh.

The agenda for the workshop was divided into three headings which would become very familiar as the debate continued:

1   Machinery for servicing a process with the status of a constituent assembly

2   Participants and remit

3   Implementation of agreed scheme

It was agreed that Greg McCarra would draw up a paper incorporating the points emerging from the Agenda Conference, the re-call Convention and the Saltire House seminar. It was intended that the paper should be circulated in early 1984, and that responses should be invited.[100]

These formal discussions were not the only ones taking place on the development of the Convention proposal. Both Hugh Miller and Paul Scott recall meeting with Jim Boyack in Scott's home in late 1983 to discuss how momentum could be added to the Agenda Conference process.[101]

Island Home Rule

Given the political depths plumbed in June 1983, the CSA approached the end of the year in relatively high spirits. The Agenda/Inter Party process seemed to hold out some prospect for progress. It was reported to the AGM held on 17 September that the CSA had sixty affiliated organisations.[102]

In the summer of 1983 the Montgomery Committee of Inquiry into the functions and powers of the Islands Councils of Scotland was taking evidence. The Committee was part of a wider review of the 1975 Scottish local government restructuring. The CSA decided to make a submission based around two points:

1   When an Assembly is established, each of the island groups should be separately represented by at least one member.

2   Given their geographic position, the islands councils should enjoy a wider range of powers than those assigned to other Scottish councils.[103]

This was an early argument for both Shetland and Orkney being directly represented in a future Scottish legislature by a member of their own. This was an argument that won the day and Orkney and Shetland, once a combined constituency, each have a member in the Scottish Parliament.

Orkney and Shetland rejected the Assembly proposed in 1979 more emphatically than any other part of Scotland. Geography and a distinctive Norse heritage fuelled the belief that Orcadians and Shetlanders would be better served by Westminster than by an Assembly dominated by the proverbial Edinburgh lawyers and Glasgow councillors. The engagement of Orkney and Shetland politicians over a period of years was important in achieving consensus within the Constitutional Convention.

Devolution Lives!

In late 1983 I was working in Edinburgh, and Jim Boyack persuaded me to accompany him to the Royal College of Physicians on 21 November where the BBC was recording a St Andrews Day debate on the proposition that:

'Devolution is dead and should be laid to rest'.

It was a clash of the Titans. Teddy Taylor opened for the proposition while John Smith led for the opposition, Nicholas Fairbairn summed up for the anti-devolutionists while Donald Dewar summed up the case for change. Other speakers included Ludovic Kennedy, Andrew Neil, Michael Forsyth, Gerry Malone, Alex Kitson, Winnie Ewing, David Penhaligan and Lionel Daiches.

The proposition was demolished with Donald Dewar outstanding. I was glad that I had accepted Jim's invitation. The political prospects for 1984 suddenly seemed a little brighter.

NOTES AND REFERENCES

[1] P.D. Lindley, *Civil Service College Working Paper No.4. The Scotland Act in Parliament. A Chronological Summary*, 1978, p.8

[2] Scottish psephologists Bochel and Denver estimated that, on a 60% turnout, 67% of those voting would have to support the Assembly in order to clear the '40%' hurdle. Quoted in the *Scotsman*, Thursday 13 February 1979, p.9

[3] Frances Wood in Ian Donnachie, Christopher Harvie, and Ian Wood (eds.) *Forward! Labour Politics in Scotland 1888-1988*, p.116

[4] John Bochel, David Denver and Allan Macartney (eds.), *The Referendum Experience, Scotland 1979*, p.6

[5] Quoted in Jim Sillars, *Scotland: A Case for Optimism*, p.65

[6] For an account of Sillars' Scottish Labour Party, see Henry Drucker, *Breakaway: The Scottish Labour Party*, 1978

[7] Henry Drucker and Gordon Brown, *The Politics of Nationalism and Devolution*, 1980, p.121

[8] Bochel et al, *The Referendum Experience*

[9] *Scotsman*, 5 January, 1979, p.7

[10] Ray Permain, 'Devolution Referendum Campaign of 1979', in H. M. Drucker and M.L. Drucker (eds) *Scotish Government Yearbook*, 1980, p.58

[11] *Ibid*

[12] Cairns Craig, 'Scotland Ten Years On. The Changes that took place while Rip Mac Winkle Slept', *Radical Scotland*, Edinburgh, Issue No. 37, February/March 1989, p.8

[13] John Kerr, The Failure of the Scotland and Wales Bill, in H.M. Drucker

and M.L. Drucker (eds.) *Scottish Government Yearbook*, Paul Harris Publishing, Edinburgh, 1978, pp.113-118

[14] Permain, 'Devolution Referendum Campaign of 1979', pp.53/54

[15] For an early salvo in this battle see Ken Coates (ed.) *What Went Wrong: Explaining the Fall of the Labour Government*, Spokesman, Nottingham, 1979

[16] Jack Brand, 'A National Assembly', in *Crann Tara*, no.13, Spring 1981, p.15

[17] Isobel Lindsay in correspondence with the author, August 2000

[18] Hugh Miller in discussion with the author, May 2000

[19] *Ibid*

[20] List of key attenders, identified in discussion with Hugh Miller, May 2000, in correspondence with Isobel Lindsay, August 2000 and in Andrew Marr, *The Battle for Scotland*, Penguin Books, 1992, London, pp.195/196

[21] Discussion with Hugh Miller in May 2000, and in correspondence with Isobel Lindsay in August 2000

[22] Marr, *The Battle for Scotland*, pp.195/196

[23] Discussion with Hugh Miller, May 2000

[24] Correspondence from Hugh Miller to Graham Salmond, dated 24 January 1980

[25] In *The Battle for Scotland* Andrew Marr wrongly identifies the Assembly Rooms in George Street as the venue for the launch.

[26] See Chris Baur in the *Scotsman* 1 March 1980, *The Weekend Supplement*, p.4 and the *Glasgow Herald* 29 February 1980, p.6

[27] *Scotsman*, 3 March 1980, p.5

[28] Resolution presented to the inaugural conference of the Campaign for Scottish Assembly on 1 March 1980

[29] *Scotsman*, 3 March 1980, p.5

[30] CSA. Minutes of the National Committee, held on 13 March 1980

[31] CSA. Notice of the Glasgow conference, held on 18 May 1980

[32] Baur, *Scotsman*, 1 March 1980, *The Weekend Supplement*, p.4

[33] CSA. Minutes of the National Committee meeting, held on 22 April 1980

[34] *Scotsman*, 30 June 1980, p.5

[35] *Ibid*

[36] *Glasgow Herald*, 21 November 1980, p.6

[37] James Mitchell, *Strategies for Self-Government. The Campaigns for a Scottish Parliament*, Polygon, Edinburgh, 1996, pp.125/126

[38] *Ibid*

[39] CSA. Minutes of the Glasgow Branch meeting, held on 11 June 1980

[40] CSA. Minutes of the National Committee meeting, held on 22 May 1980
[41] CSA. Edinburgh Branch leaflet publicising The Festival of the People, held on 28 June 1980
[42] *Scotsman*, 30 June 1980, p.5
[43] Alan Lawson in discussion with the author, August 2000
[44] *Scotsman*, 30 June 1980, p.5
[45] *Ibid*
[46] CSA. Notice of the National Conference, held on 29 November 1980
[47] CSA. Leaflet publicising the St Andrews Day Festival of the People, held in Glasgow on 30 November 1980
[48] CSA. Review of St Andrews Day Festival of the People, dated 3 December 1980
[49] CSA. Leaflet published spring 1980
[50] CSA. Invitation to the National Convention, held in the Assembly Rooms, George Street, Edinburgh on 28 March 1981
[51] CSA. Agenda for the National Convention, held in the Assembly Rooms, George Street, Edinburgh on 28 March 1981
[52] *Scotsman*, Monday 23 January 1981, p.11
[53] *Scotsman*, Thursday 26 March 1981, p.15
[54] *Scotsman*, Friday 27 March 1981, p.1
[55] *Scotsman*, Monday 30 March 1981, p.1
[56] *Ibid*
[57] *Ibid*
[58] *Scotsman*, 23 January 1981, p.11
[59] Mitchell, Strategies for Self-Government, pp.101/102
[60] Jack Brand, 'A National Assembly', in *Crann Tara* No.13, Spring 1981, Crann Tara publications, Aberdeen, p.15
[61] *Glasgow Herald*, 25 June 1981, p.15
[62] *Ibid*
[63] Billie Fraser in discussion with the author, June 2000
[64] *Sunday Standard*, No.20, 6 September 1981, p.15
[65] Quoted in the *Sunday Standard*, No.39, 17 January 1982, p.15
[66] *Scotsman*, Friday 30 October 1981, p.10
[67] CSA. *Blue Print for Scotland: A Discussion Paper*, Edinburgh, 1981
[68] *Ibid*
[69] *Glasgow Herald*, Monday 15 February 1982
[70] *Scotsman*, Monday 22 March 1982. p.10
[71] *Radical Scotland*, Issue No.1, Edinburgh, Summer 1982
[72] *Scotsman*, Monday 22 March 1982, p.10

73 *Ibid*
74 CSA. 'The Way Ahead', Declaration presented to the Second National Convention held in March 1982
75 CSA. Minutes of the National Committee meeting, held on 8 February 1982
76 *Glasgow Herald*, 18 March 1982, p.9
77 *Ibid*
78 *Sunday Standard*, No. 63, 4 July 1982
79 *Radical Scotland*, Issue No.2, Edinburgh, Autumn 1982
80 *Radical Scotland*, Issue No.3, Edinburgh, February/March 1983
81 *Sunday Standard*, No.64, 11 July 1982, p.1
82 *Glasgow Herald*, Tuesday 14 December 1982, p.3
83 *Glasgow Herald*, Thursday 9 September 1982, p.1
84 *Ibid*
85 CSA. Press statement dated Monday 13 December 1982
86 *Ibid*
87 CSA. Chair's report to the National Committee, dated 11 December 1982
88 CSA. Jim Boyack's report to the National Committee, February 1983
89 CSA. Financial Appeal, launched 27 November 1982
90 *Glasgow Herald*, Thursday 10 March 1983, p.3
91 *Scotsman*, Monday 11 April 1983, p.5
92 Figures taken from 'The 1983 General Election in Scotland', J.M. Bochel and D.J. Denver in *The Scottish Government Yearbook 1984*, David McCrone (ed.), Unit for the Study of Government in Scotland, Edinburgh, 1983.
93 CSA. *The Constitutional Convention: Proposals.* Paper submitted by Greg McCarra to the National Committee, dated 11 May 1983
94 CSA. Press release dated 13 June 1983, announcing the Agenda Conference taking place on 9 July 1983
95 CSA. Notes on the proceedings of the Agenda Conference, held in the North British Hotel, Edinburgh on Saturday 9 July 1983
96 *Ibid*
97 Letter from Helen Liddell, General Secretary of the Scottish Council of the Labour Party, dated 13 December 1983
98 CSA. Notes on the proceedings of the Agenda Conference, held in the North British Hotel, Edinburgh on Saturday 9 July 1983
99 Joint communique issued following the CSA Agenda Conference on 9 July 1983

[100] CSA. Agenda for the Constitutional Convention workshop, held on 3 December 1983, in Saltire House, Edinburgh
[101] Interview with Hugh Miller, May 2000
[102] CSA. National Committee report to the Annual General Meeting, held on 17 September 1983
[103] CSA. Submission to the Montgomery Committee of Inquiry into the functions and powers of the Islands' Councils of Scotland, dated 30 August 1983

CHAPTER 3

Preparing for Doomsday

1984 to June 1987

The Inter Party Initiative

CAMPAIGNING GOT OFF TO an early start in 1984. Following the encouraging Agenda Conference, the CSA established an Inter Party Forum which met for the first time in January. The organisations that had attended the Agenda Conference sent senior delegations to the Forum. They included Alex Salmond (SNP), Jimmy Milne (STUC), Jack Ashton (Communist Party) and Malcolm Bruce (Liberal). Jim Boyack headed the CSA contingent and Dennis Canavan was joined, in the 'personal capacity' category, by fellow Labour MP John Maxton.

The outcome of the meeting was two-fold. The represented organisations agreed to input to a joint working party, convened and serviced by the CSA, and to support a 'week of action' around the significant fifth anniversary of the March 1979 referendum.[1]

Within days of the Inter Party meeting, however, a sour note was struck in sections of the media. The decision of CSA officers to close the office in Saltire House was represented as a sign of political and organisational crisis prompted by Labour's refusal to officially participate in CSA initiatives.[2] Rebutting on behalf of the CSA, Greg McCarra insisted it was just a question of priorities and that the CSA would re-establish an office at some point in the future, 'when the time is right'.

Labour's non-participation was a political, not financial, problem. In late January/early February, the press abounded with rumours that the supposed 'ultra' devolutionists on Labour's Scottish Executive, Foulkes and Maxton, intended to raise affiliation to the CSA again, at the February 1984 meeting of the Scottish Labour Executive. Amid some of the more fevered speculation were media rumours of a

Labour take-over of the CSA designed to exclude and isolate the SNP.[3] When it came to the meeting in question, however, Foulkes and Maxton moved a resolution which accepted Liddell's earlier ruling that Labour could not affiliate to the CSA on a national, Scottish, basis. Local Labour organisations could affiliate, and the Foulkes/Maxton resolution urged Constituency Labour Parties and Branches to do so.

The CSA, in the form of National Secretary Val Marshall, responded positively, interpreting the resolution as support for the Campaign, and calling on Labour Party members to get involved in the Referendum Anniversary Week of Action.[4] In the cold light of dawn, however, the Labour decision meant that the party remained outwith the Joint Working Party.

An insight into senior Labour attitudes towards cross-party action can be gleaned from a major interview granted by Donald Dewar, then Shadow Secretary of State, to *Radical Scotland*. In the February/March 1984 issue of the nationalist/left periodical, Dewar questioned whether any 'easy kind of formal structure' (to campaign for devolution) could be built. Dewar questioned whether there was any common understanding among the parties as to the form of home rule desired, and pointed to 'divisive side-issues' raised by other parties, which he believed were intended for the Labour Party to be beaten over the head with.[5]

Dewar prohibited official Labour involvement with the Joint Working Party, and the early discussions on the Constitutional Convention which were at the heart of its agenda. Doing nothing, however, was not a credible alternative. If Dewar was to keep his 'ultras' at bay, he had to have an alternative initiative.

On 28 February 1984 the CSA circulated an early draft of the Constitutional Convention plan. The following day Donald Dewar and Gordon Brown fronted a major Labour Party press conference. The late Donald Dewar, Labour MP for Aberdeen South from 1966-1970, returned to Westminster in 1978 as the victor in the high profile Glasgow Garscadden by election. Dewar championed Labour's devolution proposals against the SNP's demand for independence, and came from behind to tame the rampant SNP. Garscadden was a national snapshot of where Scotland stood on devolution versus independence. As the victor of Garscadden, Dewar was awarded the accolade of 'Champion of Devolution'.

Gordon Brown cut his teeth in student politics at the University of Edinburgh, becoming Scotland's first Student Rector, i.e. the first student in any of Scotland's ancient universities to be elected by the student body to represent them on the University Court. Pre-Brown, rectors tended to be international statesmen, literary figures or media personalities. The prominence of his rectorial campaign catapulted Brown to the Scottish Executive of the Labour Party and in early 1979 he was elected to chair Labour's campaign group during the devolution referendum. It was a difficult job given that several members of the Executive, and even members of the campaign group, did not support the Party's pro-devolution position. In subsequent years Brown emerged as a senior Labour figure, and at the general election of 1983 combined the roles of Chair of the Party in Scotland and parliamentary candidate in Dunfermline East.

Trading on their credibility on the devolution issue, Dewar and Brown revealed that Labour would seek to build its own national consensus on the question by circulating a paper based on the 1978 Scotland Act, but including changes adopted by the Party since 1979.[6] Their initiative would become known as the 'Green Paper'. Its origins lay with Jim Ross. Jim had been head of the Devolution Unit in the Scottish Office under the Callaghan government and sought early retirement when the incoming Conservative government repealed the Scotland Act in May 1979. Free from civil service restraints, Ross was able to assist the Labour Party, of which he was a member. He was ideally qualified to kick-start the Labour Green Paper initiative.

The Fifth Anniversary

From its inception, the CSA had marked the anniversary of the 1 March 1979 Referendum. With the approach of the fifth anniversary in 1984, it was agreed to stage a Week of Action. An open letter calling for support was signed by Jim Boyack, for the CSA, the SNP's

Steven Maxwell, Ross Finnie, the Chair of the Scottish Liberal Party, STUC General Secretary, Jimmy Milne, and Peter Wilson of the Social Democrats. John Maxton MP signed in an individual capacity.[7]

The main focus of the Week was 1 March. Ten individuals led by Jim Boyack maintained an overnight vigil outside the Royal High School, the intended Assembly venue. At eleven o'clock on the morning of the 1st, the numbers swelled to 144, the number of Assembly Members proposed in the Scotland Act.[8] As the leader of Scotland's students, I was invited to be one of the 144, and to add my signature to a declaration calling for democracy. Others present included 7 Labour MPs, 1 Liberal MP, 1 SNP MP, plus representatives from the Communist Party, the Ecology Party and the STUC.

Jim Boyack, accompanied by CSA Secretary Val Marshall, knocked on the gates of the High School with the now familiar symbolic 'Key to Democracy', which along with the portico of Thomas Hamilton's High School was incorporated in the CSA's logo. Jim and Val then led the assembled company across Regent Road, to hand in a petition at St Andrews House. The Week of Action concluded with leafleting in Edinburgh, Glasgow, Dundee and Aberdeen.

Ever mindful of the need to take the campaign beyond Scotland, Jim Boyack, Greg McCarra and Ian Wallace travelled to London, and held a press briefing for the UK correspondents of the overseas media, at the House of Commons on 3 July 1984.[9]

The summer of 1984 was spent preparing initiatives for the autumn. Local government had been a source of opposition to devolution in the late 1970s. Having undergone root and branch reform in 1975/76 there was little appetite for yet another change, to the smaller single-tier councils, which many people regarded as an implicit result of establishing an Assembly. The fortunes of local councils, at the hands of the Tory-controlled Scottish Office, were causing influential local government figures to reconsider their position. It was therefore agreed by the CSA National Committee to organise a Local Government Conference in the autumn of 1984.[10]

Restructuring the Campaign

There was a view that the existing structure of a large National Committee, which elected a small Executive, had become unwieldy. The National Committee was meeting infrequently and the Executive had been dealing with the key issues. It was therefore agreed to recommend to the forthcoming AGM of the CSA that an Executive of six officers, and twelve ordinary members, be directly elected from the floor of the AGM.[11] There was also a view that the terminology of the senior officers positions required to be changed. The titles of 'Chairman', and 'Vice Chairman' were regarded as inappropriate in a modern progressive campaigning organisation. As the alternatives of 'chair' or 'chairperson' were regarded as clumsy or synthetic, it was agreed to change the titles to Convener and Vice Convener.

Ross Reassesses Priorties

On 15 June 1984, Jim Ross wrote to Jim Boyack questioning Labour's depth of commitment to its own Green Paper initiative. Since completing an initial draft, Ross had heard nothing further. On inquiring he was told that Keir Hardie House staff had now taken over the drafting process. Ross expressed his concern over media reports that the Green Paper would closely reflect the Scotland Act and fail to embrace the changes demanded by the experiences of the mid-1980s. Ross concluded his correspondence with Boyack, registering:

> 'a willingness to make an adjustment in the allocation of my time between the Labour Party and the CSA, substantially in favour of the latter.'[12]

On 19 September, Ross wrote to Boyack again, to report that he had just received an advance copy of the proposed Green Paper from Labour HQ. Ross reiterated his offer to put more time into the CSA, offered to draft a critique of the Labour document, and to prepare a paper for the proposed local government conference.[13]

Constitutional Convention becomes SNP policy

When the 1974-79 Labour Government's first attempt to legislate for devolution, The Scotland and Wales Bill, was talked out in February 1977, the then SNP research officer, Donald Bain, came up with a new proposition. Bain, who was married to Margaret Ewing, was an influential figure in his own right. He argued that the SNP should call for an elected assembly with the remit of reaching consensus on a form of home rule for Scotland. When the SNP parliamentary party presented the proposal at Westminster, it was dismissed as a constituent assembly designed to negotiate Scotland out of the United Kingdom.

Gordon Wilson saw merit in such a mechanism and, although it was not SNP policy, he continued to argue the case within and outwith the party. Eventually, in September 1984, with the strong support of Jim Sillars, Wilson succeeded and an elected Constitutional Convention became the policy of the Scottish National Party.[14]

The 1984 CSA AGM

The 1984 Annual General Meeting of the Campaign for a Scottish Assembly was held on 13 October in the University of Edinburgh Students Societies Centre at the Pleasance. The meeting may be remembered by those in attendance for the discussion on the refinement of the Constitutional Convention proposal, the report on the Inter Party initiative, or constitutional amendments. More likely they will remember the spat between George Foulkes and Jim Sillars.[15] From their respective perspectives, Foulkes and Sillars had supported the CSA from its launch. In May 1979, however, Labour's Foulkes had defeated Sillar's attempts to hold on to his South Ayrshire seat for his Scottish Labour Party. There was no end of bad blood between them and this spilled over at the CSA AGM when they shared a platform in the open discussion session.

I remember that particular AGM for my own reasons. From the summer of 1982 to the summer of 1984, I served as the elected head of the National Union of Students, Scotland. While I ensured that the NUS supported the CSA politically and practically, the nature of my duties did not allow me to put in the personal time I would have wished. I had first met Jim Boyack in 1980, and that political relationship was underlined by my working relationship with his daughter, Sarah, and son Graham, in the Labour student movement. As soon as I demitted office in August 1984, Jim engineered my co-option to the CSA Executive, and I was elected in my own right at the 1984 AGM. At that AGM I was introduced to Jim Ross and was instantly struck by his authority on the Scottish constitutional question. Prior to that AGM, I had met Alan Lawson on a couple of occasions, and like me he was elected to the CSA Executive on that day. He approached me at the conclusion of the AGM to say that he intended to make the CSA a political priority and urged me to do likewise. It was the beginning of my real involvement with the CSA, and the start of a close collaboration with Jim Boyack, Hugh Miller, Greg McCarra, Stewart Donaldson, Eric Canning, Paul Scott and of course Alan Lawson.

Val Marshall intimated her resignation as Secretary to the AGM. It took most of us by surprise and there were no immediate volunteers to take on this most important position. The issue was remitted by the AGM to the new Executive. Following discussion, it was agreed that Hugh Miller should combine the roles of Vice Convener (one of three) and National Secretary. It was also agreed that I should assist by taking responsibility for the production and distribution of members' newsletters, in a role I continued to play right through to the dissolution of the Campaign in 1999.[16] Later, Brian Duncan joined the National Executive and indicated his willingness to take on the onerous post of Secretary. He succeeded Hugh Miller in November 1986.

Hugh Miller

Originally from Perthshire, Hugh Miller's work as a sales agent for a manufacturer of horticultural and agricultural machinery led to his being in Hamilton on that fateful day in November 1967 when Winnie Ewing won her historic by election victory. Hugh remembers being in the Burgh Yard as the work force returned from lunch, many of them enthusing over the fact that they changed their voting allegiance. Within months, Hugh joined the SNP.

Hugh remained in the SNP until the 1979 referendum, but was critical of the party's less than wholehearted support for a Yes vote. During 1979 and 1980 he was involved in launching the CSA, particularly in Edinburgh (see Chapter 2). Hugh was a member of the CSA/CSP National Executive for most of the Campaign's existence, and served tours of duty as Vice Convener and Secretary. Always on the nationalist left, Hugh represented the John MacLean Society in the formation of the CSA. In the late 1980s Hugh joined the original Scottish Socialist Party, not to be confused with the Tommy Sheridan Mark II version.

Following the dissolution of the CSP, Hugh rejoined the SNP in May 1999. He believes that the return of a SNP majority in the Scottish Parliament is the best chance of achieving the independence for Scotland that he has consistently supported.

Local Government Initiative

Local government's opposition to the creation of a Scottish Assembly in the late 1970s has already been referred to, and it was only natural that the Campaign would address this source of opposition. Several senior members of the Campaign were employed in local government, and two of them, Jim Boyack and Eric Canning, took a particular interest in this initiative. Accordingly, the CSA conference, 'An Assembly and Scottish Local Government', was held in Glasgow City Chambers on Saturday 24 November 1984.

An impressive twenty four councils were represented. Of particular significance were the delegations from Shetland and Strathclyde.[17] Shetland's opposition to devolution has already been discussed. Strathclyde Region contained more than 50% of Scotland's population within its boundary and little happened within Scottish local government without Strathclyde's support. Equally impressive were the speakers at the conference, Dr Arthur Midwinter and Councillor Charles Gray.

When I arrived at the doors of the Politics Department at the

University of Aberdeen in 1975, Arthur Midwinter was already something of a legend. Having completed his studies in Aberdeen, he had moved on to the University of Strathclyde and was recognised as an academic authority on local government. From the mid-70s on, Midwinter maintained that Scotland's Regional Councils were better placed than an Edinburgh assembly to devolve real power to the Scottish people.

The 'Godfather' and 'Mr Fixit' are just two of the names by which Councillor Charles Gray, Leader of Strathclyde Regional Council, was popularly known. Charlie Gray's presence was a sure indication that a re-think was underway in Scottish local government's attitude towards a Scottish Assembly. In the years ahead Gray's readiness to engage new thinking rocked the atrophied sections of Scottish Labour.

The CSA's initiative is acknowledged as part of the process which led Scottish local government to drop its opposition to home rule. That development was confirmed in October 1986, when the Convention of Scottish Local Authorities voted by a margin of four to one to support the establishment of a Scottish Assembly.[18]

With due respect to the CSA, Strathclyde, Shetland, Arthur Midwinter and Charles Gray, the most significant influence in 'turning' local government on the home rule question was Margaret Thatcher. Under the Tory cosh, Scottish councils were well aware that the Scotland Act would have created a buffer between the Conservatives and the Councils.

'More Important'

In November 1984, the CSA co-operated with *Radical Scotland* in placing questions in the regular Systems3 opinion survey at a cost of £250.[19] The CSA's question was designed to measure the level of priority the Scottish people accorded to the creation of an Assembly. Systems3 asked respondents if they regarded the setting up of an Assembly as 'more important', 'less important' or 'about the same' compared to how it had been in 1979. The results were:

'More Important'	54%
'Less Important'	14%
'About the Same'	15%

Other questions in the survey suggested that a majority favoured an Assembly with a wider range of powers than those included in the Scotland Act.[20]

Responding to the Green Paper

In late September the CSA National Executive established a small working party to respond to the Labour Party's Consultative Green Paper on devolution. Chaired by Jim Boyack the group took the critique prepared by Jim Ross as its starting point.[21] The working party met from November 1984 to January 1985, and no less than four different drafts were produced before the final response was approved in late March 1985.[22]

The CSA's support of the principle of home rule, as opposed to the details of a particular scheme, was a fine balancing act. The CSA response to Labour's document was set within the 'constitutional logic' of the scheme, but also attempted to progress thinking on the financing of an Assembly and electoral systems. The CSA argued that the stability of any annual block grant could be guaranteed by an advisory exchequer board and the assigning of taxes to the Assembly in proportions specified in primary legislation.

When it came to identifying mechanisms for resolving disputes between an Assembly and Westminster, the CSA suggested the Judicial Committee of the Privy Council.

On the contentious issue of electoral systems, the CSA did not challenge the Green Papers's assumption that any future Assembly would be elected by first-past-the-post. Rather, it suggested that an Assembly, once elected, should have the powers to decide on how it should be elected in the future.[23]

Convention in the Public Domain

Having signed off on Labour's Green Paper, the CSA had to deal with another document, its own paper on the composition and remit of a constitutional convention. Following extensive finessing within the CSA Executive, at special workshops and among affiliated members and CSA branches, it was time to launch the proposal among Scotland's political class and see if it would sink or swim. Before letting go, however, the CSA Executive decided to subject the latest draft to another round of discussion and constructed a Referendum Anniversary event under the slogan 'Towards a Constitutional Convention'.

The event was held in Glasgow's Allan Glen's School on 2 March 1985. The morning session was devoted to the impact of Tory government policy on Scotland with particular reference to youth unemployment, given that 1985 was the International Year of the Child. The morning session endorsed a declaration on the woes of Thatcherism.[24] On the same day, the SNP National Council agreed to give a higher profile to its convention policy. Back at Allan Glen's the Executive's latest convention draft was approved for circulation.[25]

The CSA's caution in testing the credibility of its convention consultative paper was soon proven to be correct. Speaking to a pro-devolution resolution at Labour's Scottish Conference, one week later, the supposedly ultra devolutionist, CSA friendly, George Foulkes rubbished the Convention proposal as 'irrelevant nonsense'. It would never happen as long as the Tories were in power, and once Labour was returned it would simply be unnecessary.[26] Following the event at Allan Glen's, the CSA Executive submitted its convention proposal to two further rounds of discussion: a special Executive meeting on 1 April, and its reconvention on 15 April. In the course of those meetings it was agreed that the document should be presented as both a consultative and campaigning document. There was much discussion as to whether or not the CSA should identify a preferred structure for a convention. The majority of the Executive agreed that it should, and that it favoured Scotland's MPs forming the core of any convention. It was further agreed to describe how the convention would work under any feasible political scenario, e.g. a Labour or Conservative victory, arising from the next general election. It was also agreed that it was unrealistic to build the Regional Council elections of May 1986 into the Convention timetable.[27]

It was eventually agreed to launch the Convention paper on 16 May with a closing date of end September 1985.[28]

The document set out the following roles for a Constitutional Convention:

1   To articulate and represent the demand for an Assembly

2   To draft an agreed home rule scheme

3   To negotiate its implementation with the Westminster government

4   To arrange a necessary test of support

The document argued that a Constitutional Convention could assist a pro-devolution Labour Government, and save Westminster hundreds of hours of legislative time, by agreeing a home rule scheme in Scotland. This was an important point to stress, to head off the charge that support for a Convention implied an acceptance that the Tories were likely to win the forthcoming general election.

The document set out two possible models for the membership of a Convention. One centred on involving Scotland's MPs. The other advocated direct election. Both models argued for a role for local government, business, the trade unions and the churches.

An appendix outlined how the Convention created in Northern Ireland by a British government had operated during 1974/75. Another laid out a timetable for establishing a Convention, based on likelihood that the next general election would take place in the spring/early summer of 1987.[29]

The CSA Convention Consultative paper was circulated throughout Scotland. The Campaign Executive supported my proposal and produced a complementary campaign pack to equip our members and supporters to act as advocates for a Convention during the consultative period. The pack included a commentary on the key issues and questions, along with a check list of things to do.[30]

With the Convention paper launched at last, the CSA braced itself for reactions. In retrospect the closing date for responses, end September, was too tight. Many Scottish institutions effectively shutdown during July and August. The tight timetable was used as an excuse by organisations that did not want to adopt an official position, particularly in the run up to a general election. Despite CSA efforts to refine and finesse the consultative paper, the Convention challenged Scottish political convention. Resigning ourselves to the fact that a credible range of responses would have to wait until the result of the general election was known, the CSA looked to other initiatives for 1985 and 86.

Waiting for Godot

Having lobbied North of England MPs at Westminster, the CSA appreciated the influence of the North of England Labour movement on a future Labour government's ability to legislate for a Scottish Assembly. Accordingly, CSA representatives met with a delegation from the North East of England TUC, in Edinburgh, in July 1985. The tenor of the meeting was positive and the Regional TUC made it clear that its priority was not to block Scottish home rule, but to develop their own devolved regional agencies.[31]

Another development on the trade union front in early 1985, was the appointment of Campbell Christie to succeed Jimmy Milne as General Secretary of the STUC, with effect from January 1986. Christie was born in Newton Stewart in 1938, but the family moved to Glasgow in 1948, following the death of his father, a miner, from pneumoconiosis. Christie joined the Civil Service in 1954, and following National Service he worked in a munitions plant in Alexandria. Transferring to social security he became increasingly influential in his trade union, the SCPS. In 1972 he moved to London to work as a full-time officer of his union. A member of the Labour Party since 1965, Christie was also a member of CND.[32]

Campbell Christie was known to be pro-devolution, and to share the STUC's tradition of building broad alliances around issues. The CSA made early contact with the General Secretary-designate, in February 1985, in the form of a letter from Jim Boyack.[33] It received a warm response.[34]

Campbell Christie was not the only person heading for a big job in Scotland in the New Year of 1986. One time Tory devolutionist, Malcolm Rifkind, was a beneficiary of the Westland spat which saw Michael Hesseltine walk out of Margaret Thatcher's Cabinet. Rifkind's predecessor, George Younger, moved from the Scottish Office to Defence. The CSA demanded an immediate meeting with the new occupant at St Andrews House. Rifkind agreed to the principle of a meeting and during February and March 1986 the detail of the agenda for such a meeting was negotiated between the Scottish Office and the CSA. The CSA wanted to put three questions to Rifkind:

1 What was his attitude to the increase in support for a devolved assembly?

2 What was his own attitude to the form and powers of any Assembly?

3 Had he any ideas as to how the Scottish Office could engage in the process of building consensus around a home rule scheme?

The meeting turned out to be fruitless. Despite his pro-devolution past Rifkind retreated behind Official Tory disinterest. He repeatedly claimed that he could see no proof of an increase in support of constitutional change. We were forced to conclude that Rifkind's agreement to meet with the CSA was part of a public relations drive to portray the new Secretary of State as a politician ready to listen to opinion in Scotland.[35]

Jim Ross

Another accolade was bestowed in January 1986 when Jim Ross picked up the award for Scot of the Year, as voted by listeners to BBC Radio Scotland's Good Morning Scotland.[36]

Jim Ross had been a career civil servant for thirty years, twenty of them spent in the Scottish Office. His main interest was in land use planning, and in particular the West of Scotland Plan of the early 1970s. In 1975 he was appointed head of the Devolution Unit in the Scottish Office. During his four years in that job he developed a deep knowledge of the Scottish Constitutional question and deep commitment to Scottish home rule. When the incoming Tory government repealed the Scotland Act in 1979, Jim took early retirement.

A member of the Labour Party, Jim threw himself into various good causes. As he would often gleefully put it, he was a gamekeeper turned poacher. He was an Honorary Research Fellow with the University of Strathclyde's Centre for the Study of Public Policy, and Vice Chair of the Scottish Council for Social Service.[37]

The CSA was another beneficiary of Jim's energy and skills. As described earlier, Jim's involvement with the early stages of Labour's Green Paper had persuaded him that pressure from outwith was essential in persuading the Party to improve upon its existing position. In June of 1984 Jim wrote to Jim Boyack, outlining his desire to become more involved in the CSA. He joined the Campaign National Executive in October of that year, and later became the lynchpin of the Constitutional Steering Committee in 1988. Jim Ross was one of the architects of the Scottish Constitutional Convention, and all that flowed from it.

During 1985, Jim Ross became Chairman of the Trustees Savings Bank Depositors Association for Scotland, and ran a campaign to prevent the privatisation of that distinctively Scottish and mutual financial institution. Public opinion, and the courts, were persuaded by Jim, and the attempted privatisation was stopped in its tracks. It was for his role in that campaign that Jim was presented with an engraved Caithness goblet at the BBC's Glasgow headquarters at Queen Margaret Drive on 15 January 1986.[38]

Agreeing an Assembly

In January 1986, Colin Boyd, a keystone of the Edinburgh CSA, rejoined the National Executive. Colin offered to undertake a review of where the various political parties stood on the home rule question, mapping out areas of agreement and areas of difference. The intention of this initiative, 'Agreeing an Assembly' was to provide a starting point for the proposed Constitutional Convention.[39] Colin completed his task in the late spring of 1986, and the document was launched on 24 June. The launch of 'Agreeing an Assembly' was widely regarded by Campaign activists as the most successful press event organised to date by the CSA.[40] The immediate response from the political parties was disappointing, and the SNP, in the form of Alex Salmond and John Swinney, was the only party to formally meet with CSA on 'Agreeing an Assembly'.[41] As intended, however, the document acted as a route map once the Convention was established.

The Model Assembly

Another initiative in the early part of 1986 was the 'Model Assembly'. This was proposed with a view to demonstrating how Scottish representatives could debate Scottish issues, in Scotland, with a degree of detail and understanding absent at Westminster. Jim Boyack was the driving force behind this particular proposal, but within the National Executive there were members concerned with the credibility of such an event. Every Scottish MP, and a representative from each Scottish Council was invited to debate the closure of the Gartcosh Steel Mill on Friday 14 March 1986 in Strathclyde Region's debating chamber.

The debate was chaired by former *Scotsman* editor, Alastair Dunnett, and was attended by eight MPs, including Charles Kennedy, Dennis Canavan, George Foulkes, John Maxton and Russell Johnston, and a smattering of councillors from around the country, but no Conservatives. The CSA National Executive assessed the event as just credible, a view reflected by the broadsheet press. Given that the event had been staged to demonstrate how an Assembly could operate, the *Scotsman* commented:

'Having seen the future it would be premature to say that it works.'[42]

Youth for an Assembly

While the CSA worked to spread the case for home rule to the public, there were occasions when a degree of housekeeping was unavoidable. Such an instance raised its head as we planned for the 1986 Referendum Anniversary events. A group of students, almost exclusively from the Nationalist Clubs at Edinburgh and Heriot Watt universities, called a public demonstration in Edinburgh for 1 March, under the banner of Youth for an Assembly. At the behest of the CSA National Executive, Jim Boyack and I met with the organisers to express our concerns over the use of the Campaign's logo and standard typography, which gave the impression that they were an official component of the CSA. There was also concern that the group organisers had not sought the involvement nor support of the NUS, the CSA's main youth and student affiliate, and had organised the protest for 1 March, which clashed with a major national student event. In an attempt to move the discussion on to more positive ground, we asked the organisers to make contact with the NUS, and Jim undertook to speak to the NUS leadership to see what support it could mobilise for the march. We also agreed to urge members of the CSA's Edinburgh Branch to help swell the numbers.[43]

An estimated 400 people attended the Youth for an Assembly protest march on 1 March 1986. The majority of them were members of the CSA's Edinburgh Branch and, as a youth event, it was barely credible. It was agreed that some mechanism for involving young people in the structures of the CSA was required.[44] That task was handed to Pauline McNeill, now the MSP for Glasgow Kelvin, but in 1986 a member of the CSA National Executive. Accordingly, a structure for a 'youth aggregate' was approved at the AGM of the CSA in November 1986. The youth aggregate never really functioned in practice. This was partly due to the fact that the CSA was always something of a 'middle-aged' organisation, and partly to the Campaign priorities dictated by the changes in the Scottish political landscape following the 1987 general election.

The summer of 1986 should have been a time for celebration as Scotland and Edinburgh hosted the Commonwealth Games for a second time. In the run up to the opening ceremony, the Games were undermined by the daily withdrawal of Black Commonwealth nations protesting against what they perceived to be the Thatcher Government's soft attitude towards apartheid in South Africa. In an attempt to stem the hemorrage of teams, Campbell Christie led a group of 'prominent Scots' to London, to lobby high commissions and make it clear that the British Government's attitude to apartheid was not reflected in Scotland.

Alan Lawson, representing *Radical Scotland*, was part of the delegation, and although it was unsuccessful in the short-term, it proved significant in the longer run. It demonstrated that Campbell Christie was prepared to exercise his authority, as the leader of a significant sector of Scottish society, in the Scottish national interest. On the return flight from London, Alan Lawson and another member of the delegation found themselves on the same flight as Secretary of State Malcolm Rifkind. Alan was particularly impressed by the way in which his colleague tackled Rifkind during the journey home. The articulate lobbyist was Canon Kenyon Wright.[45]

Scottish Business and the London Media

The CSA rounded off 1986 with initiatives aimed at sectors of Scottish society not usually associated with support for home rule. In November of 1986 the CSA held a lunch for prominent Scottish business figures with the aim of splintering the commercial sector's monolithic opposition to constitutional change.[46] This early business approach involved Alan Armstrong, who would later become the CSA's National Convener.

The first CSA press conference in London was held on 1 December 1986 at the headquarters of the SCPS trade union. Alan Lawson set out the case for devolution as a forerunner for wider decentralisation in the United Kingdom as a whole. Jim Boyack outlined the growth in the CSA, citing the increase in the number of affiliated organisations, including local authorities.[47]

While the press conference was well covered by the Westminster correspondents of the Scottish broadsheets, the London press stayed away. It was a reminder, if one was needed, of the difficulties in convincing the London-based media to focus on developments in Scotland.[48]

The Declaration Dinner

The first CSA event of 1987, general election year, was the Declaration Dinner held in Edinburgh's Caledonian Hotel on 27 February. The evening was modelled on the great reform banquets of the 18th and 19th centuries, which rallied radicals in the cause of democracy.[49] The speakers for the evening were Chris Harvie, Kay Carmichael and, at the suggestion of Alan Lawson, Kenyon Wright.[50]

Those attending the Dinner were asked to endorse the following declaration:

> 'We believe that the time has come when Scotland must assume control over her own affairs through a democratically elected Assembly. Only by doing so can we properly develop our own skills and resources, safeguard our national culture and identity and restore a proper sense of dignity to our people. We therefore believe that the Scottish Assembly should be set up by the next government as an immediate priority.'[51]

The Declaration Dinner was the first event in yet another Week of Action to mark the 1979 referendum. Other events during the 1987 action included the targeting of local radio phone-in programmes on Sunday 1 March, the signing of a national pledge in Glasgow's George Square on Friday 6 March and leafleting in the Conservative marginal constituencies of North East Fife, Ayr, Edinburgh Pentlands and Dumfries and Galloway.[52]

Talking Doomsday

Radical Scotland heralded its 25th issue, the first of 1987, as the 'Doomsday Edition'.[53] The Doomsday Scenario was the term coined to describe the likelihood of the pending general election ending in a rout for the Conservatives in Scotland, but a Tory government being returned by an English majority. It was not unknown for a party to take control of the Scottish Office on the basis of English votes, but in early 1987 there was growing concern at the prospect of a Tory rump holding on to the keys to St Andrews House, and Dover House, with total disregard for Scottish opinion.

But how was the term coined? Back in 1986 a schools project was launched to mark the 900th anniversary of the Domesday (or Doomsday) Book, the census of English landowners and their property ordered by William the Conqueror in 1085/86. The Domesday Book did not apply to Scotland and the emergence of the school project north of the border moved Paul Scott to raise his concerns at a CSA National Executive, and propose that the CSA should launch an alternative demographic project based around Sinclair's Statistical Account, the first Scottish census compiled between 1791-8. I was of the view that our time and energy should be concentrated on the likelihood of a Tory election victory. Our main concern should be the Doomsday Scenario, not the Domesday Book. I have read different accounts as to how the 'Doomsday Scenario' entered the political vocabulary, but my memory of that exchange is clear.

NOTES AND REFERENCES

[1]   CSA. Report of the Inter Party meeting, held in Edinburgh on Saturday 7 January 1984
[2]   *Glasgow Herald*, Friday 13 January 1984, p.7
[3]   *Glasgow Herald*, Thursday 7 February 1984, p.7
[4]   *Scotsman*, Monday 13 February 1984
[5]   *Radical Scotland*, Edinburgh, Issue 7, February/March 1984, pp.7-9
[6]   *Scotsman*, Thursday 1 March 1984, p.6
[7]   CSA. Referendum Week of Action 1984
[8]   *Glasgow Herald*, Friday 2 March 1984, p.5
[9]   CSA. Report to the National Executive on the London press conference, 3 July 1984
[10]   CSA. Minutes of the National Executive meeting, dated 9 July 1984
[11]   CSA. Minutes of the National Executive meeting, dated 2 April 1984
[12]   Letter from Jim Ross to Jim Boyack, dated 15 June 1984

[13] Letter from Jim Ross to Jim Boyack, dated 19 September 1984

[14] See James Mitchell, *Strategies for Self Government. The Campaigns for a Scottish Parliament*, Polygon, Edinburgh, 1996, pp.127-130

[15] CSA. Minutes of the Annual General Meeting, held on 13 October 1984

[16] CSA. Minutes of the National Executive meeting, held on 26 November 1984

[17] CSA. Report of the Local Government Conference held on 24 November in Glasgow City Chambers

[18] James Mitchell, *Strategies for Self Government. The Campaigns for a Scottish Parliament*, Polygon, Edinburgh, 1996. p.103

[19] CSA. Minutes of the National Executive meeting, held on 11 September 1984

[20] *Glasgow Herald*, 30 November 1984

[21] CSA. Timetable for the Working Party on the Labour Party's consultative Green Paper

[22] CSA. Minutes of the National Executive meeting held, on 18 March 1985

[23] CSA. Response to Labour's consultative Green Paper

[24] CSA. All Party declaration released on 2 March 1985

[25] *Scotsman*, 4 March 1985, p.6

[26] *Scotsman*, 9 March 1985, p.4

[27] CSA. Minutes of the National Executive meeting, held on 1 April 1985

[28] CSA. Minutes of the National Executive meeting, held on 15 April 1985

[29] CSA. *The Scottish Constitutional Convention: A Consultative Paper*, Campaign for a Scottish Assembly, Edinburgh, May 1985

[30] CSA. Constitutional Convention Campaign Pack, May 1985

[31] Interview with Hugh Miller, May 2000

[32] *Radical Scotland*, Issue 15, June/July 1985, p.10

[33] Letter from Jim Boyack to Campbell Christie, dated 10 February 1985

[34] Letter from Campbell Christie to Jim Boyack, dated 26 February 1985

[35] CSA Newsletter, 'The Consensus Grows'

[36] *Scotsman*, Thursday 16 January 1986, p.8

[37] *Radical Scotland*, Issue 8, April/May 1984

[38] *Scotsman*, Thursday 16 January 1986, p.8

[39] CSA. Minutes of the National Executive meeting, held on 20 January 1986

[40] CSA. Minutes of the National Executive meeting, held on 18 August 1986

[41] CSA. Minutes of the National Executive meeting, held on 18 August 1986

[42] *Scotsman*, Saturday 15 March 1986, p.7

[43] CSA. Minutes of National Executive meeting, held on 20 January 1986

[44] CSA. Minutes of National Executive meeting, held on 17 March 1986

[45] Interview with Alan Lawson, August 2000
[46] CSA. Minutes of the National Executive meeting, held on 18 November 1986
[47] *Scotsman*, Tuesday 2 December 1986, pp.4&5
[48] CSA. Minutes of the National Executive meeting, held on 8 December 1986
[49] CSA. National Members mailing, January/February 1987
[50] CSA. Minutes of the National Executive, held on 23 February 1987
[51] Kenyon Wright, *The People Say Yes!*, Argyll Publishing, 1997, p.26
[52] CSA. National Members mailing, January/February 1987
[53] *Radical Scotland*, Issue 25, February/March 1987

CHAPTER 4

A Claim of Right

From the General Election of June 1987 to the First Meeting of the Scottish Constitutional Convention in March 1989

The Role of the CSA in the General Election of June 1987

THE CSA ANNUAL GENERAL MEETING in November 1986, held in the Golden Lion Hotel in Stirling, was an upbeat affair with all eyes fixed on the general election expected in the spring of 1987. One addition to the CSA National Executive at that AGM was Alan Smart. Alan was my immediate successor at the National Union of Students, Scotland. In the early and mid-1980s the NUS was something of a production line for the CSA. Alan's successor as President of NUS Scotland, Pauline McNeill, now an MSP, was a member of the CSA National Executive, and my own deputy from my time at the NUS was Jack McConnell. Now First Minister of Scotland, Jack graduated from student politics to Labour local government, and was a regular attendant at CSA events and a regular contributor to *Radical Scotland*.

The Annual General Meeting agreed to the calling of a special National Council of the CSA immediately following the general election, in order to allow the CSA to make an early response to the outcome. As soon as the date of the election, 11 June, was known, Saturday 20 June was set as the date for the special National Council.[1]

The CSA's intention to intervene in the forthcoming general election caused concerns among Scotland's political parties. They were worried that CSA interventions in individual constituencies could count against the election expenses of the local candidates of the pro-home rule parties. To avoid such concerns, the CSA decided not to endorse TV87, the campaign advocating tactical voting in key marginal constituencies. The decision was taken despite the efforts of Pip Hills of TV87 to persuade the CSA otherwise.[2]

Having decided against appeals for tactical voting in targeted constituencies, the Executive considered framing a declaration, or pledge, on Scottish home rule, which each of the parties would be invited to sign, thereby isolating the Conservatives. This suggestion set off its own alarm bells. The Scottish National Party would not sign any document which did not call for independence, while the Alliance parties, Liberal and SDP, refused to endorse any home rule pledge which did not make it clear that any future assembly would be elected by proportional representation.[3]

Following lengthy discussion it was agreed that the CSA should not endorse individual candidates, and should not seek the endorsement of political parties.[4] The CSA would run its own advertising, and Alan Smart took on the job of spreading the available finance as widely as possible. The advertising message was a play on the advertising slogan for a brand of Australian lager and proclaimed that the Tories didn't give a XXXX for Scottish home rule.[5] The heat generated over the CSA election intervention was much ado about very little. On the eve of the June 1987 general election, a key moment in the struggle for home rule, the total national funds of the CSA amounted to £3,500, of which the Executive decided to spend £3,000 on the advertising campaign. London advertising giants Saatchi and Saatchi grumbled legal threats over the CSA's parody, but backed off.[6] Perhaps they had some insight into the finances of the CSA and accepted that ye canna take the breechs off a Heilan' man.

During the general election, the CSA joined forces with the Saltire Society in organising a meeting on business and an assembly, in an attempt to bring candidates and business people together. One solitary candidate turned up, but the Bank of Scotland, The Scottish Council Development and Industry and Miller Construction were present. The CSA was represented by Jim Boyack and Alan Armstrong. It was another attempt to crack the perceived business monolith opposing home rule.[7]

Party Reactions to the General Election Result

The CSA National Executive met two days after the election, on 13 June.[8] From the standpoint of today, when there is one solitary Scottish Tory at Westminster, it is difficult to recall the shock created by the reduction of Tory MPs from twenty two to ten. It bestowed credibility on the 'No Mandate' argument, which challenged the legitimacy of this Tory rump to govern Scotland. As recently as 1955 the Unionists (as the Scottish Tories were known until 1964) were the largest Scottish party and captured an overall majority of Scottish votes in the general election of that year.

The shock felt by Scottish Tories was betrayed by Malcolm Rifkind's formal meeting with Labour Leader Donald Dewar, within one week of the election, to discuss how Scotland was to be governed. Rifkind was toiling to appoint a ministerial team and faced the embarrassment of suspending the Scottish Select Committee when two of the Scottish Tory awkward squad, Bill Walker and Alan Stewart, refused to serve.[9] Dewar demanded an assembly, a jobs strategy and the abandonment of the proposed Poll Tax in return for a constructive opposition.[10] While Rifkind rejected Dewar's terms, a Tory Plan B was discussed throughout the summer of 1987. 'The Way Forward Report' is reputed to have been written by Ross Harper, encouraged by Rifkind.[11] Apparently the Plan advocated implementing home rule on Tory terms: an assembly without any economic powers, and a cut in the number of Scottish MPs at Westminster.[12] As late as April 1988, ten months after the election, Tory commentator and historian, Michael Fry, addressed the Edinburgh Branch of the CSA on devolution proposals advocated by the Conservative Constitutional Reform Group.[13] Fry and his group were doomed to failure, however, as unreconstructed Tory Unionism regained its nerve.

The Tories were not the only party with problems. With a massive majority of Scottish MPs, Labour was open to the jibe of 'feeble' as it seemed incapable of preventing the imposition of Tory policies in Scotland, including the Poll Tax.

The SNP and the Liberal/SDP Alliance had little to cheer about as both under achieved on their pre-election estimates. Sparking with recrimination, the Alliance blamed their failure to break through on the electoral system and before long they were involved in an acrimonious merger.

This was the political backdrop to the Special National Council, the arena into which the CSA trooped on Saturday 20 June 1987.

The Special CSA National Council, 20 June 1987

When the CSA National Executive met on 13 June it was to consider the agenda for the Special National Council scheduled for the following Saturday in Glasgow's City Halls. The meeting failed to come to an agreement, and reconvened on the evening of 16 June.[14]

After much discussion, it was agreed that I would move an 'Agenda for Action' at the Special National Council, debate would be opened to the floor and I would conclude the meeting by replying.[15] Although the meeting took place in 1987, I remember it very clearly. The 'Agenda for Action' contained a few familiar ideas which the parties were very unlikely to take up. The central suggestion, however, was that Labour should dust off its Green Paper and present it at Westminster as an opposition White Paper. The other pro-change parties were urged to support the White Paper at Westminster to demonstrate the depth and breadth of the demand for the principle of home rule.

In moving this package, I was at pains to point out that it was expected that the SNP and the Alliance parties would move their own amendments, but we were calling on them to support the White Paper in the final vote. My point about parties moving their own amendments seemed to go over the heads of many of those present. The CSA Executive was accused of trying to manipulate the situation in Labour's interests. SNP members present complained about their party being put on the spot about voting for devolution, as opposed to independence. The fiercest opposition, however, came from the Liberals and SDP members present. Fresh from yet another general election in which they felt they had been robbed by the electoral system, they were not in the mood to support an assembly package that did not include proportional representation.[16] Fearing that the CSA's position was being deliberately misconstrued, I gave as good as I got in a relatively pugnacious reply. Media observers estimated that about one third of the 200 people entitled to vote rejected the Agenda for Action, and the *Glasgow Herald* proclaimed 'Cracks Appear in United Front for Devolution'.[17]

It had seemed right to convene the CSA within nine days of the general election, but it may not have been long enough to allow people to reflect, or to allow the hurt to heal.

In moving the Agenda, I was instructed by the CSA National Executive to put down a marker for changes within the CSA itself.[18] The general election had demonstrated the CSA's lack of resources, and if the Campaign was to meet the challenges ahead, it had to transform its finances. The most obvious way to achieve this was to increase the affiliation fees for large organisations. It was a suggestion that would impact on the way the CSA operated.

CSA *Perestroika*

From the moment Alan Smart joined the National Executive in November 1986, he maintained that the organisation was under achieving on the finances it should have been able to raise from its impressive list of major affiliated organisations. Until that point the maximum affiliation fee was £35, and that applied to major national organisations and large local authorities that counted their budgets in millions.[19] As the dust settled on the special National Council, Alan Smart became National Treasurer, taking over from Peter Findlay, who had been a stalwart of the CSA from its early days. Vice Convener, Colin Weir, one of the more senior SNP figures active in the Campaign, chose this point to resign. He was replaced by another SNP member, Alan Armstrong, who had been active on the business front since joining the CSA.[20] The Executive was further strengthened by the co-option of two Alliance 'big hitters': the Liberals' Jim Shearer and the SDP's Bernard Ponsoby. Jim's contribution was cut tragically short by a fatal car crash, and Bernard is currently Scottish Television's Political Editor.[21]

As National Treasurer, Alan Smart produced 'Getting It Together', a consultative paper on the structures of the CSA. The paper posed four honest questions to the CSA's members, affiliated and individual:

1   Was it accepted that only a vigorous campaign could make clear to the Government the strength of support for an Assembly?

2   Was it agreed that a strong, well resourced campaign, organised across party lines was required?

3   Could such an organisation grow out of the CSA?

4   Were members, particularly affiliates, prepared to resource such an organisation?[22]

If the answer to all four questions was yes, affiliated organisations had to be given a greater role in the CSA. Until this point every individual member was entitled to attend the CSA AGM and National Conference and vote, while the country's largest local authority, encompassing more than half of Scotland's population, was entitled to two votes. 'Getting It Together' proposed that individual members should be represented through local CSA Branches with one vote for every ten members, while the maximum entitlement of the largest affiliates would be capped at six. Affiliation fees would be calculated by a formula based on membership or, in the case of local authorities, population.[23]

Members were asked to respond by the end of August 1987 with a National Council debate on 10 October and AGM decisions on 28 November. While there was general agreement that the CSA had to increase its resources, there were concerns that a greater role for affiliated organisations would overshadow the influence of individual members and increase the influence of the Labour Party. The CSA National Executive's response was 'Transforming the CSA: A Summary of Responses'.[24] The document demonstrated what the delegate entitlement to CSA AGM and National Conference would look like under the proposed system of representation:

Local Authorities	46
National Organisations	48
Local Organisations	59
CSA Branches	60
National Executive	18

Sixteen of the delegates from local authorities would be representing non-Labour Councils, while twelve of the trade union delegates, included under National Organisations, would be representing unions that were not affiliated to the Labour Party. The paper also outlined what would happen to the CSA's income if the changes went ahead. It was projected that the annual income from affiliation fees would rise from £2,850 to £9,700.[25] In the long run the increase in the CSA's income proved even greater than the advocates of change predicted. In the eight months from 1 January to 31 August 1988, the CSA's income was £12,553 compared to £4,985 in the whole of 1987.[26]

From the Festival of Democracy to the CSA AGM on 28 November 1987

While Alan Smart was busy persuading the Campaign to back the re-organisation plans, the other 'Alans', Lawson and Armstrong, represented the CSA on the Committee organising The Festival for Scottish Democracy.[27] The Festival was a STUC initiative to demonstrate the breadth of support for home rule. Before we gathered on Glasgow Green, however, the event seemed in danger of unravelling. The statement which participants had to endorse referred to home rule 'within the UK' a phrase which effectively forced the SNP to withdraw, and the Alliance parties followed them complaining that their invitation to participate had been half-hearted.[28]

Perhaps the brightest aspect of the day was the sticker produced by the CSA for the event, emblazoned with the figure 78%, the overwhelming majority of Scottish people who had voted for parties advocating constitutional change at the 1987 general election. It was unfortunate that we were unable to accommodate the representatives of the 78% within the one big tent on Glasgow Green. On the positive side, the event demonstrated Campbell Christie's readiness to support cross-party initiatives.

The re-organisation of the CSA was a piece of complex political choreography. The National Council of the CSA met (for the last time) on 10 October 1987 and discussed the responses to the consultation exercise, and an AGM of the Campaign was held in the Grosvenor Hotel in Edinburgh on 28 November 1987. Given the complex changes involved, the meeting ran very smoothly and the Executive's recommendations were carried. The existing Executive was re-elected en bloc with the mandate of organising another AGM, on the basis of the new constitution, as soon as possible.

The first AGM under the new structure took place in Stirling's Albert Hall on 27 February 1988.[29] Immediately following that meeting, several Labour Party home rulers made their way to Jack McConnell's flat in Stirling and established what became known as Scottish Labour Action.

As early as September 1987, Jim Boyack informed the CSA National Executive that he would not be seeking re-election as Convener. A life-long home ruler, Jim was a founder member of the CSA, had served as its Convener for five years and was synonymous with the CSA in the minds of many people. As the CSA was re-organising, Jim was reassessing his own role. This included a round of discussions with senior colleagues. Speaking thirteen years after the event, Alan Lawson recalls that there was a view that changing circumstances demanded outstanding communication skills, and that those could be best provided by Alan Armstrong.[30] Jim concurred but by no means was it the end of his commitment to the CSA. He continued to bring the enthusiasm and energy that marked his Convenership to the CSA National Executive.

Alan Armstrong had a marketing company of his own, and some pretty definite ideas on corporate identity. Having elected Alan to succeed Jim in February 1988, the CSA approved a new logo. Out went the Royal High School portico and the key of democracy and in came a new dynamic design suggesting a reinvigorated Campaign.[31]

Following the AGM, Isobel Lindsay was co-opted to the Executive. Like Jim Boyack, Isobel was a founder member of the CSA and had stayed in contact with the Campaign ever since, making her the most senior SNP figure consistently involved in the CSA.[32]

On the way out, however, was Alan Smart. After working as a teacher for a few months, Alan secured a new job as a researcher with Scottish Television's Current Affairs department, which ruled out frontline or high profile political activity. Alan chose a career in television and is now Head of Broadcasting for the Scottish Parliament. Alan Smart was succeeded as Treasurer by banker and Labour Party member Alan Milnes. Alan's expertise served the CSA during a period in which its finances were transformed.[33]

Another key decision taken at the 1987 AGM was the approval in principle of a new initiative to revive the Constitutional Convention proposal – the Constitutional Steering Committee.[34]

The Constitutional Steering Committee

The CSA launched its consultation on a Constitutional Convention in May of 1985, with a closing date of end September, but the low number of responses was disappointing. The Convention proposal was placed on the 'back burner' until the autumn of 1987. In an attempt to kick-start the Convention project, Alan Lawson presented a paper to the October 1987 meeting of the CSA National Executive, seeking agreement to raise the matter at the forthcoming AGM.[35] The paper was the fruit of discussion between Alan Lawson and Jim Ross.

Alan called for the appointment of a Constitutional Steering Committee consisting of 12-15 prominent people, representing a wide cross section of Scottish life, to revisit the Convention question and report on its membership and remit. Alan pointed to the fact that Labour's Green Paper, which had been a feature of the Scottish political scene since the summer of 1983, was likely to be presented at Westminster, and rejected, prior to the end of 1987. This would create a vacuum that the Convention could fill, and the endorsement of a range of prominent Scots would increase the Convention's prospects.[36]

While the CSA AGM approved the idea in principle, discussion on the detail continued in the Executive, and there was a concern that the CSA was handing over responsibility for the Convention to another body.[37] These fears were mostly calmed by the assurance that the Steering Committee would report to the CSA and that members of the Executive would sit on the Steering Committee.[38] Jim Ross, the obvious choice as Secretary to the Steering Committee, argued that it had to be independent of the CSA, and to that end he would resign from the CSA National Executive while he served as Secretary to the Steering Committee.[39] It was finally agreed that two members of the CSA National Executive would sit on the proposed Steering Committee, and Paul Scott and Isobel Lindsay, both members of the SNP, were nominated.[40] During December 1987 and January 1988, Alan Lawson, and other senior CSA figures, recruited people prominent in different walks of Scottish life to serve on the Steering Committee.

The establishment of the Constitutional Steering Committee was announced at a press conference held at Edinburgh's Sheraton Hotel on 11 February 1988. The press conference was fronted by Alan Armstrong, as Convener of the CSA, and Sir Robert Grieve and Jim Ross as Chair and Secretary of the CSC.[41] The other members of the Constitutional Steering Committee were:

Bill Anderson	Scottish Secretary of the National Federation of the Self-Employed and Small Business
Ian Barr	Senior Executive with the Scottish Post Office Board
Rev. Maxwell Craig	Church of Scotland Church and Nation Committee
Sandra Farquhar	Worker with Scottish Women's Aid in Stirling
Nigel Grant	Professor of Education, University of Glasgow. Labour Party

Joy Hendry	Editor of *Chapman*, and literary critic
John Henry	Retired Deputy General Secretary of the Scottish Trade Union Congress. Labour Party
Pat Kelly	Assistant Scottish Secretary of the National Union of Civil and Public Servants. Labour Party
Isobel Lindsay	Lecturer in Sociology, CSA appointee. Scottish National Party
Neil MacCormick	Leading lawyer, son of John MacCormick. Scottish National Party
Una Maclean McIntosh	Lecturer in Community Medicine. Widow of John P. McIntosh. Labour Party
Paul Scott	Former diplomat, writer, and CSA appointee. Scottish National Party
Judy Steel	Cultural events organiser, wife of David Steel. Liberal Democrat

Derek Barrie, the Liberal Democrat Convener of North East Fife District Council, and Rev. Dr Joseph Devine were appointed to the Constitutional Steering Committee but resigned prior to it beginning work.[42]

With the Constitutional Steering Committee established and working, the CSA returned to other initiatives in the spring of 1988. With the increase in affiliation fees working its way through the system, and a grant of £1,500 from the Joseph Rowantree Reform Trust, the Campaign was in a position to re-establish an office and, for the first time, appoint a paid, part-time worker.[43] An office was rented at Ruskin House in Edinburgh's Windsor Street, a property owned by the Edinburgh City Labour Party. Other tenants included various trade unions and a spiritualist church. The first organiser, appointed in April 1988, was Gillian Gloyer, a recent graduate and a leading young Liberal Democrat. Gillian found full-time employment relatively quickly and, in August 1988, she was replaced by Labour Party member Steve Condie.[44] On 'Democracy Day', 11 June 1988, the anniversary of the general election, CSA members delivered leaflets in nine targeted parliamentary constituencies. The CSA's cross-border links continued with Jim Boyack attending a conference of the Campaign for a Welsh Senate.[45]

Largely as a result of Jim Ross' stewardship, the Constitutional Steering Committee completed its remit in good time. On 6 July 1988 'A Claim of Right for Scotland' was presented to the CSA. There had been two previous Claims of Right. In 1689, when the Scottish Parliament rejected King James VII and II, and in 1842 when the Free Church of Scotland split with the Church of Scotland. The 1988 'Claim' was set in the Scottish historical and constitutional tradition that dated all the way back to Declaration of Arbroath in 1320. The logic of the 'Claim' was as follows. Scots in 1707, and since, assumed that the Union with England guaranteed certain aspects of Scottish identity, including the church and the law. The 'Claim' concluded that, as old assumptions were no longer being fulfilled there was a need for a Constitutional Convention. The Claim also included proposals on the membership and remit of a Convention.[46]

The publication of the Claim had an immediate impact on the language of the home rule debate. It outlined that the old Scots legislature, which came to an end in 1707, had been called 'parliament' and that modern proposals for home rule had also preferred the term parliament. It therefore concluded:

'There are good arguments for returning to the traditional usage of 'parliament' rather than 'assembly' but this is a matter that should be considered by the Constitutional Convention.'[47]

The CSA had consistently used the formula 'assembly or parliament' when referring to a Scottish legislature. Following the publication of the Claim, the term 'assembly' was used less and less. The CSA, however, retained the term 'assembly' in its title for a further four years.

Sir Robert Grieve

The Constitutional Steering Committee was chaired by the late Sir Robert Grieve, who died in 1996. Robert Grieve had been Emeritus Professor at the University of Glasgow and a former chief planner with the Scottish Office. He was appointed as Chair of the Highlands and Islands Development Board under Labour Secretary of State, Willie Ross, and also served as chair of the Royal Fine Art Commission for Scotland. Among an array of other academic posts and public offices, Sir Robert was chair of an important study into Glasgow's housing.

Sir Robert Grieve believed that central government controlled planning in Scotland through its control of the economic agenda. As a result, the most important planning decisions in Scotland were not accountable to her chosen political representatives. This was the basis of Sir Robert's support for home rule, and for a Scottish Parliament with meaningful economic powers.

Reactions to A Claim of Right for Scotland

'A Claim of Right for Scotland: The Report of the Constitutional Steering Committee' was unveiled to Scotland's media on the morning of Wednesday 13 July in the Roxburghe Hotel in Edinburgh's Charlotte Square. For a document now regarded as the intellectual basis of Scottish home rule, its publication was not universally heralded. Scottish Television's news coverage ignored the Claim totally. BBC Scotland's coverage was regarded as 'selective and misleading' while the *Daily Express* editorial was 'virulently hostile'.[48]

Labour's response was led by Shadow Secretary of State for Scotland, Donald Dewar, who maintained that Labour was only interested in initiatives that could make progress and that was the test the Party would apply to the CSC report. Looking ahead to the proposed Constitutional Convention, Dewar said:

'There will be concern about the remit of an ad hoc body which is to act as a focus of resistance and political negotiation.'[49]

Also from the Labour ranks, General Secretary Murray Elder lobbed a potential time bomb, telling the media that it would be 'virtually impossible' for Labour in Scotland to agree a response until the next Scottish Labour Conference in March 1989.[50] Elder's statement was released during the CSA press conference and was probably the most difficult ball Alan Armstrong had to juggle with on that morning.

Undeterred by Elder, the CSA swung into the largest-ever campaign of consultation and persuasion in its entire history. In the course of August to December 1988 the CSA met with a host of organisations and key individuals, including:

Councillor Charles Gray, Labour Leader of Strathclyde Regional Council

Scottish Trade Union Congress

Each of the seven largest trade unions affiliated to the STUC

Convention of Scottish Local Authorities

Scottish Council of Churches

National Union of Students

Scottish Liberal Democrats

Social Democratic Party

Scottish National Party

Communist Party

Green Party[51]

All of the meetings went well, with the notable exception of that with the Convention of Scottish Local Authorities (COSLA), which was represented by Jean McFadden and Eric Milligan, both of whom had been Labour No campaigners back in the 1979 devolution referendum. The doubting duo argued that COSLA's members would find difficulties with the principles of the Claim and the proposed time table for the convening of a Convention. They even suggested that some local councils would quit COSLA if it backed a Claim of Right.[52] While Milligan and McFadden demonstrated disinterest, the world's media was keen to learn what was going on in Scotland in the summer of 1988. The CSA was contacted by French television, the *New York Times*, the *Los Angeles Times* and RTE. There were also approaches from the Campaign for a Welsh Assembly (formerly Senate), the Flemish Christian Union and other 'regionalist' movements across Europe. An approach from Edinburgh University Press resulted in the Claim being published as a book including accompanying essays edited by leading pro-home rule academic Owen Dudley Edwards.[53]

Brian Duncan

The frenzied round of activity and meetings was co-ordinated by Brian Duncan, who served as CSA National Secretary from 1986-1992.

The CSA/CSP embraced a range of motivations and opinions. For Brian, the Campaign was about better government, rather than Scottish national aspirations. Not surprising perhaps from a political scientist and a graduate of Aberdeen, Strathclyde and Sheffield universities.

Brian joined the Labour Party in 1978 and his initial experience of the CSA was the Edinburgh Branch. Brian was co-opted to the National Executive with a view to eventually succeeding Hugh Miller as Secretary. During his time as Secretary, Brian held down a day job with the National Health Service Common Services Agency. Brian resigned and withdrew from CSA/CSP in late 1992, over strategic disagreements on the Campaign's direction following the Tory general election victory earlier that year. (see Chapter 6)

Labour's Road to Convention

By the time Alan Armstrong penned an update for the autumn 1988 issue of *Radical Scotland*, he was able to announce official SNP and Liberal Democrat support for the Claim and the Convention. The STUC General Council had unanimously endorsed the report and even COSLA, so hostile a matter of weeks earlier, appeared likely to back the Claim when its Executive met on 30 September, as did the Scottish Council of Churches. There was also progress to report on the Labour Party front. Labour had launched an internal consultation exercise with a closing date of 1 November 1988. Meeting with a CSA delegation, Murray Elder indicated that if the outcome of the consultation was clear then the Party's Scottish Executive might feel able to agree a response in November, rather than wait until March 1989.[54]

While the CSA had lobbied Labour hard, there were other pressures that led to a modification of the Party's initial response to the Claim. During the summer of 1988 the recently established Scottish Labour Action, and others, had called on the Party to lead a campaign against the hated Community Charge or Poll Tax. The flat rate tax, for local services, did not feature in the Tories 1987 Scottish Manifesto, and the unfair nature of the proposal ran counter to Scotland's egalitarian tradition. The Government's decision to impose the Poll Tax in Scotland ahead of the rest of the United Kingdom was a classic example of the mis-government of Scotland so forensically dissected in A Claim of Right. The debate came to a head with a recall conference of Labour in Scotland at Govan Town Hall on 17 September 1988. The leadership line of ruling out non-payment as part of the campaign was carried, but the call for non-payment was boosted by the support of the Transport and General Workers Union.[55] The pressures on the Dewar/Elder leadership from CLP activists, the STUC, and sections of Labour local government intensified when Labour Leader, Neil Kinnock, decided to appoint former Secretary of State for Scotland, Bruce Millan, to the European Commission. This created a by election in the historically volatile Glasgow Govan constituency. The SNP's candidate was Jim Sillars.

Sillars was the leader of the Scottish Labour Party, which split with Labour in 1975; he was married to Margo MacDonald, who had captured the seat for the SNP in a dramatic by election in 1973. The by election was set for 10 November 1988.

The first sign of a senior Labour shift of policy, on the Claim and the Convention, was spotted by Ewan Macaskill, the political correspondent of the *Scotsman*, as Labour figures arrived in Blackpool for their UK Conference. Under an 'exclusive' tag in the *Scotsman* of 3 October 1988, Macaskill reported on an interview with Donald Dewar in which the Scottish Labour leader said:

'... if there is a chance to find common ground which will unite Scottish opinion that is a prize of considerable importance.'[56]

On 21 October, Dewar amplified that view in the Andrew Williamson Memorial Lecture at Stirling University. John Smith was to have delivered the lecture, but Dewar stepped in when his friend suffered a heart attack.[57] Dewar chose the occasion to welcome the Liberal Democrats' decision not to insist on proportional representation as a pre-condition to a Convention. Dewar went on to say:

'The people must decide if they are prepared to live a little dangerously in order to achieve what they want.

It means that the Labour Party must be prepared to negotiate, and not simply seek to enforce the devolution package that we already have before the public.'[58]

Twenty days later SNP champion, Jim Sillars, overwhelmingly defeated Labour in Govan. Two days later, Labour's Scottish Executive agreed to endorse 'A Claim of Right', and to attend preliminary cross-party talks on the establishment of a Constitutional Convention.

At the time, and since, argument has ranged over whether or not Labour would have come on board without the electoral pressure of Govan. The by election took place on 10 November 1988. As early as 2 October, Dewar had signalled his readiness to move his position, and underlined that view on 21 October. Labour's internal consultation closed on 1 November and it was on the basis of those responses that the Executive decided on 12 November to 'live a little dangerously'. Understandably, Nationalist critics have sought to challenge the precise choreography by arguing that the writing was on the wall for Labour in Govan long before polling day. Chris Harvie may have it about right when he argues that Labour's decision to engage in the Convention process was not a direct result of the by election, but that 'such a formidable opponent (Sillars) in the ring concentrated Labour minds'.[59]

Whatever the impact of Sillars' victory on Labour, it had greater implications for the Scottish National Party.

Trying to Keep the SNP On Board

During the Govan campaign Sillars struck a relatively conciliatory tone on the question of cross-party initiatives, and while the SNP favoured a directly elected Convention, there was an assumption it was an opening marker in any future negotiation. The mood changed with Sillars' victory and a subsequent improved position in opinion polls putting the SNP within 4% of Labour at 32%.[60] On 11 December the SNP Executive tied its participation in the Convention process to direct elections, or a link with the European Parliament elections scheduled for June 1989.[61] At an Executive away weekend, on 14/15 January 1989, the SNP rejected the suggestion afloat in Scottish political circles that David Steel might chair the proposed Convention.[62] The SNP confirmed its position of linking Convention membership to the forthcoming European elections. Seduced by their own opinion poll rating, they believed that such linkage would produce a Convention with an SNP majority.[63] The SNP did agree, however, to accept the CSA's invitation to talks based on 'A Claim of Right' on the understanding that they were exploratory at that stage.[64]

The All Party Talks of 27 January 1989

The meeting to discuss the Claim took place on Friday 27 January in the COSLA headquarters in Edinburgh. The meeting was convened by the CSA, as the commissioners of the Claim, and was represented around the table by Convener Alan Armstrong, Vice Convener Alan Lawson and National Secretary Brian Duncan. Sir Robert Grieve chaired the first part of the proceedings in his capacity as Chair of the Constitutional Steering Committee. His committee had fulfilled its remit, and the Claim was now the property of the CSA.

The SNP had three representatives, Gordon Wilson, Margaret Ewing and Jim Sillars. The five-strong Labour delegation was led by the late Donald Dewar and included Scottish Chair and Vice Chair, Esther Quinn and Mark Lazarowicz, Ernie Ross as convener of the Scottish Parliamentary Labour Group, and Party General Secretary Murray Elder, who was returning to work following a heart and lung transplant. The Liberal Democrats also had five representatives, led by their Scottish Leader Malcolm Bruce MP. The Convention of Scottish Local Authorities, the largest delegation, was led by Eric Milligan. The Scottish Trade Union Congress was represented by Campbell Christie while the Scottish Council of Churches was represented by Canon Kenyon Wright.[65] The main strand of Scottish opinion not represented at the talks was the Conservative Party and its business allies. A chink of light broke through in the days following the all party talks when Scottish Affairs Committee of the National Federation of the Self Employed and Small Business voted to seek representation in a future Convention.[66] This small breakthrough was largely thanks to the influence of Bill Anderson, the Federation's Secretary, who had served on the Constitutional Steering Committee and subsequently the CSA National Executive.

The exploratory talks at the COSLA headquarters lasted for four hours amid a media frenzy which veteran commentators described as the largest Scottish political press event since the height of the devolution debate of the mid-1970s.[67] Although no recording of the event exists, it is generally accepted that the SNP negotiators pressed three points:

A Convention primarily based on MPs elected at the 1987 general election would under-represent the post-Govan SNP, which was regularly registering 32% in the opinion polls.

The Convention should assert the sovereignty of the Scottish people.

That any agreement reached by the Convention should be tested by a multi-option referendum along with other constitutional options, including independence.

Labour's response was crucial. Surprisingly perhaps, Donald Dewar was prepared to contemplate a SNP 'top-up' and the involvement of SNP councillors was discussed. While ringing declarations of sovereignty sounded awkward to many Labour politicians, they realised that they had already effectively accepted Scottish sovereignty by agreeing to meet on the basis of the Claim. The main sticking point was the SNP demand for a referendum at the end of the Convention process. Labour, and others, argued the SNP proposal ran counter to the goal of agreeing a home rule scheme by consensus. In an attempt to reassure the Nationalists, Dewar reiterated that a Convention would only proceed by consensus, and that there would be no question of the SNP, or any other party, having the unacceptable foisted upon it by a majority vote.[68]

The meeting concluded with the SNP agreeing to participate in a six-person business committee, chaired by Kenyon Wright, while they reported back to their National Executive and ultimately to their National Council on 4 March.[69] The SNP negotiators emerged up-beat from the 27 January talks. Questioned by the media, the CSA's Alan Armstrong said he would be 'very disappointed' if the SNP decided not to participate in the Convention.[70]

SNP leader, Gordon Wilson, claimed that on the Friday evening of the 27 January talks he was inundated by calls from Party colleagues opposing participation in a Convention. This reaction led him to ring around senior SNP office bearers. All of those he contacted expressed opposition to involvement in the Convention process. It was on that basis that he decided to use his speech at a Burns Supper in the Edinburgh SNP Club to distance the SNP from the Convention. Wilson attacked the proposed composition of the Convention as 'a travesty of reality'.[71] This interesting process of policy-making by Burns Supper was followed, on Monday 30 January, by a statement from the three SNP negotiators, Gordon Wilson, Margaret Ewing and Jim Sillars to the effect that they would be recommending against joining 'Labour's rigged Convention.'[72] Those present at the talks, and those waiting off stage for news, reported that Jim Sillars had seemed both positive and conciliatory, and were surprised when Sillars fell in line with Wilson. It may well be that Margo MacDonald, who at that time harboured great distrust of the Labour Party and devolution schemes, influenced her husband's thinking.

Interestingly, Alex Salmond, then Deputy Convener of the SNP, has consistently claimed that he was not contacted by Wilson over the weekend of 28/29 January 1989, and has criticised the course of action followed by the Party.[73]

If Salmond had been kept out of the loop, and nursed reservations about the wisdom of Wilson's strategy, he kept those feelings to himself. Open opposition to the Wilson line was confined to a couple of constituency associations, the former Party President, and first SNP Member of Parliament, Dr Robert McIntyre, and two CSA associates, Neil MacCormick and Isobel Lindsay, both of whom had served on the Constitutional Steering Committee. Isobel responded to the negotiators' statement with a paper in which she argued that the SNP was exposing itself to accusations of putting pursuit of party advantage before Scotland's interest.[74] Compelling as Isobel's arguments were, her proposal to join the Convention could not find a seconder at the SNP National Executive meeting held on 11 February. Another proposal, to continue participation in the Business Committee meantime, was defeated by a margin of twenty three votes to six.[75]

Calls on the SNP to enter the Convention came from a variety of sources. Appeals by Labour home rule enthusiasts, George Galloway, John McAllion, Willie McKelvy, Dennis Canavan and Campbell Christie were ignored.[76] On 28 February a last ditch meeting was held at Westminster. The Labour Party was represented by Donald Dewar and John McAllion; Jim Wallace and Malcolm Bruce represented the Liberal Democrats, while the SNP were represented by Margaret Ewing and Jim Sillars. Canon Kenyon Wright was present in his role as chair of the Business Committee. The SNP pair raised the same three issues: membership, sovereignty and a referendum that had dominated discussion on 27 January.[77] Concessions on membership and sovereignty were confirmed. As any referendum would not happen until the end of the Convention process, it was suggested that the SNP could participate in the Convention while discussion continued on the principle and detail of any referendum.[78]

Ewing and Sillars reported back, but the promise of continuing discussions on a referendum was not enough. A request that Kenyon Wright should address the SNP National Council, meeting in Port Glasgow on Saturday 4 March, was rejected.[79] The SNP National Council consisted of less than three hundred people, its meeting on 4 March was attended by six hundred. A resolution supporting SNP involvement in the Convention process was defeated by one hundred and ninety eight votes to forty eight, and Isobel Lindsay was viciously heckled when she spoke.[80] Margaret Ewing described the decision to remain outwith the Convention as 'a demonstration of political astuteness' and Alex Salmond accused Isobel of being 'more Unionist' than both the Secretary of State for Scotland and Labour's Charles Gray.[81] To his credit, Salmond has since expressed regret at the way Isobel was treated and his own role in leading the charge.

It did not take long for Isobel's interpretation of where the people of Scotland were it to be proven correct. In January 1989, two months after Govan, the SNP scored an all time high poll return of 32%, but by late February support for the SNP had slipped to 24%.[82]

The following weekend, Labour's Scottish Conference assembled in Inverness and voted overwhelmingly to back the Convention process, a move endorsed by Party Leader Neil Kinnock. As Professor James Mitchell has put it:

'United behind involvement in the Convention (Labour) was able to exploit the divisions within the SNP. Labour had outmanoeuvred the SNP, recaptured the mantle of 'Scotland's national party' lost only three months before, exploited divisions within the SNP and was able to present the Nationalists as sectarian to the public. Labour politicians could not believe how easy it had been.'[83]

Making policy by Burns Supper is not to be recommended. While efforts were being made to keep the SNP on board, the CSA continued its role of preparing for the inaugural meeting of the Scottish Constitutional Convention planned for 30 March 1989. It was under CSA convenership that issues such as standing orders, the role of COSLA, and the topping up of delegations were agreed. It was also agreed that the CSA would act as the Convention's banker, both raising and administering the Convention's funds.[84] The CSA was to have three seats in the Convention and Alan Armstrong, Alan Lawson and Isobel Lindsay were appointed.

Following meticulous preparation, the Scottish Constitutional Convention, a central objective of the Campaign for a Scottish Assembly since its inception on 1 March 1980, finally met on 30 March 1989 in the Assembly Hall of the Church of Scotland on the Mound in Edinburgh.

In its Convention preview the Glasgow *Herald* acknowledged the role played by the CSA, describing the moment as the 'culmination of almost ten years of sustained pressure'.[85] The *Scotsman* ran with a page one picture of Alan Armstrong with the empty, yet expectant, chairs of the Conventioneers ranked behind him.[86] David Steel and Harry Ewing were elected as Co-Chairs of the Convention, and the founding statement, crafted to ensure broad support, was signed by fifty eight of Scotland's seventy one MPs, by seven of Scotland's eight members of the European Parliament, by representatives of fifty nine of Scotland's sixty five local authorities and seven political parties, including the Orkney and Shetland movements.[87]

Many great words were spoken on the Mound on 30 March 1989, but the most memorable were those uttered by Kenyon Wright. Wright was elected as Chair of the Convention's Executive, which included representatives of the Labour Party, the Liberal Democrats, the Communist Party (soon to be restyled as the Democratic Left), the Green Party, COSLA, the STUC, Small Business, the Churches and of course the CSA.[88] Paraphrasing Prime Minister Thatcher's assuming of the 'Royal We', Wright posed the rhetorical question:

'What if that other single voice we know so well responds by saying, 'We say No, and we are the State.' Well, we say Yes, and we are the People!'[89]

Spirits were running high in the ranks of the CSA on that early spring day, although there were those SNP members who faced the dilemma of divided loyalties. On the morning of 30 March 1989, the headline of the *Scotsman* editorial called it correctly:

'Now for the hard bit.'[90]

NOTES AND REFERENCES

[1] *Radical Scotland*, Issue 27, June/July 1987, p.5
[2] CSA. Minutes of the Executive Committee meeting, held on 23 March 1987
[3] CSA. Minutes of the National Executive Committee meeting, held on 15 May 1987
[4] *Ibid*
[5] *Ibid*
[6] CSA. Minutes of the National Executive Committee meeting, held on 29 June 1987
[7] *Glasgow Herald*, Friday 5 June 1987, p.3
[8] CSA. Minutes of the National Executive Committee meeting, held on 13 June 1987
[9] Iain MacWhirter, 'After Doomsday... The Convention and Scotland's constitutional crisis', in *The Scottish Government Year Book 1990*, Alice Brown and Richard Parry (editors), Unit for the Study of Government in Scotland, Edinburgh, 1990, pp.23 and 24
[10] *Scotsman*, Friday 19 June 1987, p.1
[11] Alan Lawson 'Mair nor a rauch wind blowin...' in Alice Brown and David McCrone (editors) *The Scottish Government Yearbook 1988*, The Unit for the Study of Government in Scotland, pp.40 and 41
[12] *Ibid*
[13] CSA. Notification of the Edinburgh Branch meeting held on 23 April 1988, with Michael Fry as guest speaker
[14] CSA. Minutes of the National Executive meeting, held on 13 June 1987
[15] CSA. Minutes of the National Executive meeting, held on 16 June 1987
[16] *Glasgow Herald*, Monday 22 June 1987. p.3
[17] *Ibid*
[18] CSA. Minutes of the National Executive meeting, held on 13 June 1987
[19] *Radical Scotland*, Issue 28, August/September 1987

20   CSA. Minutes of the National Executive Committee meeting, held on 14 July 1987

21   CSA. Minutes of the National Executive Committee meeting, held on 29 June 1987

22   CSA. *Getting It Together: A Consultative Paper*, July 1987

23   *Radical Scotland*, Issue 28, August/September 1987

24   'Transforming the CSA. Summary of Responses', dated 24 September 1987

25   *Ibid*

26   CSA. Minutes of the National Executive meeting, held on 14 July 1988

27   CSA. Minutes of the National Executive Committee meeting, held 6 August 1987

28   *Ibid*

29   'CSA: Organising the Re-organisation'. Paper presented to the National Executive Committee meeting, dated 15 September 1987.

30   Alan Lawson in discussion with the author, August 2000

31   CSA. Minutes of the National Executive Committee meeting, held on 26 October 1987

32   CSA. Minutes of the National Executive Committee meeting, held on 21 December 1987

33   CSA. Minutes of the National Executive Committee meeting, held on 11 January 1988

34   *Scotsman*, 31 November 1987, p.15

35   CSA. Minutes of the National Executive Committee meeting, held on 26 October 1987

36   CSA. Strategy in 1988. Paper presented by Alan Lawson to the National Executive Committee meeting in October 1987

37   CSA. Minutes of the National Executive Committee meeting, held on 2 November 1987

38   *Ibid*

39   CSA. Minutes of the National Executive Committee meeting, held on 11 January 1988

40   *Ibid*

41   CSA. Press release dated Thursday 11 February 1988

42   'A Claim of Right For Scotland: Report of the Constitutional Steering Committee', Edinburgh, July 1988

43   CSA. Minutes of the National Executive Committee meeting, held on 10 May 1988

44   CSA. Minutes of the National Executive Committee meeting held on 9 August 1988

[45] CSA. Minutes of the National Executive Committee meeting, held on 14 June 1988

[46] Owen Dudley Edwards (editor), *A Claim of Right for Scotland*, Polygon, Edinburgh, 1989

[47] A Claim of Right, Edinburgh, July 1988

[48] CSA. Minutes of the National Executive Committee meeting, held on 14 July 1988

[49] *Scotsman*, Thursday 14 July 1988, p.2

[50] *Glasgow Herald*, Thursday 14 July 1988, p.1

[51] Progress report to CSA National Executive Committee meeting, dated 2 September 1988.

[52] Reported to the CSA National Executive Committee on 9 August 1988

[53] CSA. Minutes of the National Executive Committee meeting, held on 19 December 1988

[54] See *Radical Scotland*, Issue 35, October/November 1988, p.4

[55] *Glasgow Herald*, Thursday 14 July 1988, p.1

[56] *Scotsman*, Monday 3 October 1988, p.1

[57] *Glasgow Herald*, Saturday 22 October 1988, p.3

[58] *Scotsman*, Saturday 22 October 1988, p.1

[59] Christopher Harvie, *Scotland and Nationalism: Scottish Society and Politics 1707 to the Present* (Third Edition), Routledge, London, 1998, pp.26-28

[60] Iain MacWhirter, 'After Doomsday... The Convention and Scotland's Constitutional Crisis' in Alice Brown and Richard Parry (Editors) *The Scottish Government Yearbook 1990*, Unit for the Study of Government in Scotland, 1990, pp.26-28

[61] *Scotland on Sunday*, 11 December 1988, p.2

[62] *Scotland on Sunday*, 15 January, 1989, p.2

[63] *Radical Scotland*, Issue 38, April/May 1989, p.11

[64] *Scotland on Sunday*, 15 January, 1989, p.2

[65] For a breakdown of the delegates see *Scotsman*, Friday 27 January, p.5

[66] *Scotland on Sunday*, 29 January 1989, p.2

[67] *Glasgow Herald*, Saturday 28 January 1989, p.1

[68] Kenyon Wright, *The People Say Yes!*, Argyll Publishing, 1997, pp.42/43

[69] *Scotsman*, Saturday 28 January 1989, pp.1&2

[70] *Glasgow Herald*, Saturday, 28 January 1989, p.3

[71] *Scotsman*, Monday 30 January 1989, p.3

[72] *Scotsman*, Tuesday 31 January 1989, p.1

[73] Alex Salmond speaking in the documentary *The Salmond Years*, Scottish Television

74 *Glasgow Herald*, Wednesday 1 February 1989, pp. 1&3
75 *Glasgow Herald*, Monday 13 February 1989, p.1
76 *Scotland on Sunday*, 5 February 1989, p.2
77 *Scotsman*, Wednesday 1 March 1989, p.1
78 *Scotsman*, Thursday 2 March 1989, p.4
79 *Scotsman*, Friday 3 March 1989, p.4
80 Scotsman, Monday 6 March 1989, p.1
81 *Glasgow Herald*, Monday 6 March 1989, p.18
82 *Ibid*
83 James Mitchell, *Strategies for Self Government. The Campaigns for a Scottish Parliament*, Polygon, Edinburgh, 1996, p.129
84 CSA. National Executive Committee meeting, held on 15 March 1989
85 *Glasgow Herald*, Thursday 30 March 1989, p.1
86 *Scotsman*, Thursday 30 March 1989, p.1
87 Andrew Marr, *The Battle for Scotland*, Penguin Books 1992, pp.204-206
88 Kenyon Wright, *The People Say Yes!*, Argyll Publishing, 1997, pp.124/125
89 *Ibid*, p.52
90 *Scotsman*, 30 March 1989, p.10

CHAPTER 5

Towards Scotland's Parliament

April 1989 to June 1992

Agreeing a Scheme

BY THE TIME OF the Scottish Constitutional Convention's second meeting, in Inverness on 7 July 1989, its Executive had established a series of working parties dealing with the difficult questions any serious home rule scheme had to answer. They included the powers and functions of a Scottish Parliament, the financing of home rule, and the future constitutional relationship of Scotland with the rest of the United Kingdom, e.g. Scottish representation at Westminster and the entrenching of the Scottish Parliament. The Executive also established an Islands' Committee to address the concerns of the sparsely populated areas most distant from Edinburgh. It was also part of the ongoing process of binding Orkney and Shetland into the home rule project.[1]

Two other working parties were also established. The Women's Issues group represented Scottish women's demand for fair representation in the government of the new Scotland. It was easier to make such demands of a 'green field' political institution without sitting members and vested interests. The remaining working party, looking at participation and public support, was established in line with the section in the Claim calling on the Convention to build support for an agreed home rule scheme among the Scottish people.[2]

If there were any lingering doubts that the SNP had suffered for its decision to boycott the Convention, they were dispelled on 15 June 1989 when Labour's Mike Watson saw off a challenge from the SNP in the Glasgow Central by election. Six months earlier, in the immediate wake of the Govan result, the SNP would have been odds on favourite to pull off a victory. The disputes over the Convention, however, had transformed the post-Govan landscape.

A Different Role

The convening of a credible Constitutional Convention had been a CSA objective since the Campaign was established in 1980, and an over-riding priority since the 1987 general election. Now that the Convention was working, the CSA had to reassess its own role during the eight months, seven full Convention meetings, fifty Executive and Working Party meetings and two rounds of national consultation that it took to produce the first home rule scheme.

As referred to earlier, the CSA acted as the Convention's banker. Relative to the sums of money the CSA had been used to administering on an annual basis this represented a major responsibility that was handled expertly by CSA Treasurer Alan Milnes. As an example of the sums involved, Alan reported that in the first six months of the Convention's existence, the CSA had paid COSLA £6,000 for administrative and printing costs incurred on behalf of the Convention, and that further COSLA bills amounting to £3,500 were expected soon.[3]

In September 1989, Steve Condie, the CSA's full-time administrative assistant, was offered a job with the BBC. It was anticipated that once the Convention scheme was agreed, the Convention itself would move into Campaign mode, and applications for funding that phase had already been submitted by the CSA. In those circumstances it was agreed not to refill Steve's position until the Convention's campaigning structures were clarified and agreed.[4]

Another change in the CSA hierarchy was signalled in the autumn of 1989 when Convener Alan Armstrong informed the National Executive that he would not be seeking re-election come the next CSA Annual General Meeting planned for February or March 1990.[5] Alan's stated reason for stepping down as Convener was the difficulty in balancing the responsibilities of the post with the demands of an Economics degree course which he had signed up for at Heriot Watt. There is little doubt, however, that Alan, as a SNP member, was disappointed by the party's refusal to join in the Convention.

Within the Convention, the CSA's role was that of facilitator and honest broker, rather than advocate for any particular proposal. The scheme being sketched out by the Convention, however, reflected several propositions which had evolved from CSA thinking through-out the previous decade. These included a parliament based on pow-erful cross-party, pre-legislative committees which would counter bal-ance Executive domination and patronage.[6] On the question of a post-home rule Scotland's position within the UK, the CSA sought to inform the debate with international comparisons. In December 1989 the CSA proposed, organised and funded a Scottish delegation to Euskadi, the Basque Country. From the perspective of 1989, the Spanish system of autonomous regions operating different degrees of home rule seemed a useful model for a situation in which Scotland went first and furthest.

The CSA suggested and funded the delegation. Chris Ross, an activist in the Edinburgh Branch, and lecturer in Spanish at Heriot Watt, organised the trip and acted as interpreter and guide to the delega-tion.[7] The delegation included Kenyon Wright, Bob McCreadie, the Liberal Democrats' leading negotiator in the Convention, and CSA Convener Alan Armstrong. Scotland's media was represented by the *Glasgow Herald's* Murray Ritchie, and Peter Jones, then political editor with the *Scotsman*. The other member was Welsh home rule campaigner John Osmond, who joined the delegation in Euskadi wearing his hat as a correspondent with *Wales on Sunday*. From 12-17 December 1989, the delegation visited Vittoria, Bilbao, San Sebastien, Guernica and Durango to meet with Basque politicians, civil servants, employers and trade unionists. They visited the Basque Parliament and were received by the Basque Lehendaraki or premier.[8]

As part of the CSA's ongoing efforts to inform the rest of the UK of developments in Scotland, the Campaign joined forces with the Campaign for a Welsh Assembly, and Charter 88, in organising a conference entitled 'The 1990s: A Decade for Constitutional Change', held in Coleg Harlech over the weekend of 6/7 January 1990.[9] The CSA had been in regular contact with the Campaign for a Welsh Assembly since it first appeared on the scene as the Campaign for a Welsh Senate. Emulating the Czechoslovakian 'Charter 77' campaign, Charter 88 was established to campaign for reform of the British constitution.

The main obstruction to initial Convention agreement on a home rule scheme for Scotland was the issue of electoral systems. Should a future Scottish Parliament be elected by the traditional first-past-the-post, or by an alternative, proportional system? From the disappointments of the 1983 general election there had been a growing realisation that a new parliament had to be elected by a fair electoral system that would produce a legislature representative of Scotland as a whole. The Labour Party, Scotland's largest political party, was the main obstacle to proportional representation and it was down to people within the party to clear the roadblock to Convention consensus. This was achieved on Saturday 10 March 1990 when, on a wet Dunoon afternoon, Labour's Scottish Conference ruled out first-past-the-post as a method of electing a Scottish Parliament and adopted a set of criteria for an alternative which pointed towards the Additional Member System (AMS). This decision, carried by a margin of 372,000 to 285,000 was pivotal in allowing the Convention to reach consensus.[10] This change in Labour's position, which many commentators predicted would never happen, was due to a number of prominent trade unions, e.g. the Transport and General Workers, NUPE, the Engineers and the leadership of the STUC. In the Constituency Labour Parties the campaign for change was led by Scottish Labour Action. In July 1989, SLA launched a campaign for the Additional Member System.[11] Between then and March 1990, the subject was debated in literally hundreds of constituency and branch Labour Parties. Although a narrow majority of CLPs voted in favour of first-past-the-post in Dunoon, the shift in opinion was nothing short of a 'political earthquake'.[12]

At the close of the Conference session, supporters of PR gathered in a fringe meeting to celebrate the breakthrough. Among those on the platform was Isobel Lindsay, making one of her first speeches since being elected as Convener of the CSA the previous weekend.

Isobel succeeded Alan Armstrong as convener at the Annual General Meeting of the CSA held in Edinburgh City Chambers on 3 March 1990. Alan remained on the Executive as one of our three Vice Conveners, the others being Alan Lawson and senior Liberal Democrat Moira Craig. Brian Duncan and Alan Milnes continued as Secretary and Treasurer.

Isobel Lindsay

Isobel Lindsay's political involvement dates back to 1960 when, as a member of the Campaign for Nuclear Disarmament's 'Committee of 100', she joined early sit down protests at the Holy Loch. From that time on, she has been consistently active in the peace movement.

Isobel joined the Scottish National Party in 1967. It was a time of rapid growth and within a year she had become Secretary of the SNP's Glasgow District Association and Nationalist councillor for the previously safe Labour Dalmarnock ward. Those early days on Glasgow Corporation left her committed to community involvement and wary of political whipping and the exaggeration of differences.

Isobel was the SNP candidate in the Berwick and East Lothian by election of October 1978, a contest which marked the derailment of the Nationalists' 1970s bandwagon. Eighteen months later, Isobel was one of the people who founded the CSA in March 1980. From its inception, Isobel was the most senior SNP figure, and Scottish female activist, in the ranks of the CSA/P.

Isobel was a member of the Constitutional Steering Committee in 1988. Later she became Convener of the CSA, and represented the organisation in the Constitutional Convention.

In 1990 Isobel did not renew her SNP membership, believing that the party's opposition to the Convention was irreconcilable with her role. In 1995 she joined the Labour Party, convinced that the election of a Labour government was essential to delivering the Convention's home rule scheme. The Scottish political village was rocked in 1997 when the Labour Party rejected Isobel as an approved candidate for the first Scottish Parliament election in 1999. Her exclusion, and that of other leading women, suggests that the selection process was something more than an objective test of competence.

Isobel's current academic research at the University of Strathclyde includes Scottish graduate migration, voluntary sector leadership and Anglo/Scottish stereotypes. Away from her work at Strathclyde, Isobel is Vice Convener of the Scottish Civic Forum and Convener of the Scottish Coalition for Justice Not War. She writes regularly for a number of publications, including *Scottish Left Review*.

The Day for Scotland

In order to sustain its campaigning profile, while the Convention moved towards consensus, the CSA joined with other organisations, invited by the STUC, to organise a major event in Stirling on 14 July 1990, 'The Day for Scotland'.[13] For a number of years the CSA had aspired to get leading Scottish musicians, with a mass following among Scotland's young people, to associate themselves with the home rule cause, but with limited results. In the summer of 1990, however, the higher profile of the issue, the credibility of the STUC, and contacts within the Scottish music business, ensured the event was a media success and was much enjoyed by the thousands who attended. The organisation of rock concerts on green field sites is an expensive business and, despite the terrific turnout, many months were to pass before the books were closed on 'The Day For Scotland'.

Preparing for the Campaign Phase

In the summer of 1990 it was anticipated that the Constitutional Convention would unveil its consensus scheme in October of that year. Thoughts were therefore turning to the appointment of a Convention Campaign Director whose job would be to organise the public promotion of the Convention scheme in the run up to the next general election, which was widely expected to take place in the summer or autumn of 1991. The post was funded by money from the Joseph Rowantree Reform Trust, which had successfully been applied for by the CSA in its capacity as the Convention's banker. The CSA National Executive also agreed to fund the costs of a part-time Deputy Director, and to pay an honorarium to Kenyon Wright in recognition of the amount of time he was devoting to Convention business and the home rule cause generally. It was agreed to provide the Convention Campaign Director with a budget of £7,000 for materials etc., part of his remit being to raise additional funds.[14]

Early in September 1990 Harry Conroy was appointed as Convention Campaign Director. Former business correspondent with the *Daily Record*, Harry had just completed a stint as General

Secretary of the National Union of Journalists in London. As his CV indicates, Harry has excellent communications skills, and is very well connected with the Scottish Labour movement, an important factor given his responsibility to raise additional campaign funds.[15] Church of Scotland minister, Kathy Galloway, was appointed Deputy Director. Unfortunately, Kathy had to resign within a few months for family reasons. Her post was never filled.

Thoughts were also turning to the content of the campaign. Former CSA Convener, Alan Armstrong tabled a campaign strategy, covering the period September 1990 to April 1991, at the CSA National Executive Committee meeting in July 1990. Alan was a marketing professional who had run his own company, and his paper was detailed and comprehensive.[16] Alan estimated the costs of the campaign at £100,000 (at 1990 prices) and he argued that £75,000 should be contributed by the political parties supporting the Convention. While no one doubted the effectiveness of Alan's proposed plan, there were many doubts about expecting Labour, the Liberal Democrats and the smaller parties in the Convention to stump up £75,000 with a general election on the horizon. Up to that point, the total cash donated to the Convention by political parties, as opposed to support in kind, was just £2,000. Alan's response was that the commitment of the Convention parties to campaign for their own home rule scheme had to be tested.[17]

At the August meeting of the CSA National Executive, Isobel reported that she, with the backing of the other office bearers, had presented an edited version of Alan Armstrong's marketing plan to the Convention Executive. She had done so in the belief that the full set of proposals would be regarded as unachievable. Unfortunately, this incident led to Alan Armstrong tendering his resignation from the post of Vice Convener, and from the National Executive, on 23 August 1990.[18] In his resignation letter Alan argued that the Convention was content to secure party commitments in election manifestos and was not serious about running an effective campaign in the interim. As a result of Alan's departure, Brian Duncan took his place as one of three CSA representatives in the Convention, while Doug Chalmers of the Communist Party replaced him as a Vice Convener.[19]

Alan Armstrong and Jim Boyack

While working in London in 1962/3, Alan Armstrong joined the Scottish National Party. On returning to Scotland to work for the Scottish Tourist Board, he was unable to be politically active as STB employees were regarded as civil servants. Deeply disappointed by the result of the 1979 referendum, Alan quit the STB and set up his own marketing agency. A business associate introduced him to Hugh Miller who wasted no time in introducing Alan to the Edinburgh Branch of the CSA. Alan was a polished performer and his rapid rise through the ranks of the CSA was due to a widely held view that Alan possessed the skills to represent the CSA when it occupied centre stage in 1988/89.

The circumstances behind Alan's resignation have already been discussed and he has always argued that he was in no way compromised by his membership of the SNP. Indeed Alan is no longer a member of the SNP as he parted company with the party on account of its Euro enthusiasm.[20]

In the late summer of 1990 the CSA suffered a cruel loss when Jim Boyack died unexpectedly on Friday 31 August. That afternoon I was due to travel to St Andrews for a weekend get together for first time Labour parliamentary candidates and their election agents. I was Eric Clarke's election agent in Midlothian, and it was in that capacity that I headed to Fife. Before setting off at lunchtime, I received a call from Alan Lawson to break the dreadful news. Throughout the journey to St Andrews I kept recalling memories of Jim. I always regarded myself as being doubly connected with Jim. On the one hand he was a Labour Party comrade and fellow home ruler, but he was also the devoted Dad of Sarah and Graham with whom I had worked very closely in Labour youth and student politics. On arriving at my destination, I met up with Wendy Alexander, who at that time was the Labour Party's Scottish research officer. It was a beautiful late-summer day and I will always remember Wendy commenting on the contrast between the weather and the gloom which had descended upon us.

Jim Boyack was a Dundonian, and his own family research revealed links with the jute trade. He trained as an architect. Later he would make a mid-career switch to town planning. He was a member of the Royal Town Planning Institute and was working with the former Strathclyde Regional Council at the time of his death.

Jim Boyack was a lifelong Scottish home ruler. He had been 'out' in the Covenant movement of the late 1940s/early '50s, a track record that made many of his colleagues feel like Johnny, or Jenny, come lately. Jim served as a Labour Councillor on Edinburgh Corporation. He should have gone on to serve at a more senior level but, in the Labour Party of the 1960s and 70s, his views on home rule, fair votes and Europe were too far ahead of their time.

Jim was a founder member of the CSA in 1980, became convener in 1983 and served in that post until early 1988. His good nature and determination sustained the CSA in the difficult times of the early 1980s.[21]

The Jim Boyack Memorial Project

The desire to create a memorial to Jim led to the Jim Boyack Memorial Project in 1991. Given Jim's interest in architecture and planning, the CSA agreed that a suitable tribute would be an exhibition and publication on the development of the Royal High School campus on Calton Hill, the proposed site for a Scottish Parliament. With financial support from the National Union of Civil and Public Servants, McGregor Associates, a clutch of supportive architects, interior designers, photographers, sculptors, and with Alan Lawson managing for the CSA, the project addressed three objectives:

1   to ensure public access to the Parliament
2   to provide media facilities
3   to enhance the appearance and surroundings of the existing
     building[22]

The exercise produced two main sets of proposals:

A   The building of a new modern public reception area, or 'Tryst',
     on the west of the site. There members of the public could

meet with elected representatives, access public information and follow the proceedings of the Parliament on closed circuit television.

B   The conversion of a sports centre on the east side of the site into a state of the art media centre.[23]

When it came to enhancing existing buildings, the project team suggested a range of possibilities. They included an underpass linking the Parliament with St Andrews House, the creation of an exhibition area in the undercroft, stone cleaning, floodlighting and a series of enhancements to the portico of the former High School, which research had revealed to have been the original intention of its architect Sir Thomas Hamilton.[24]

The exhibition toured in early 1992, and the accompanying brochure was widely distributed. If Jim Boyack was ahead of his time, so was the memorial project. It raised issues about the Parliament's home which would resurface with a vengence in 1997.

Initial Consensus

The Scottish Constitutional Convention met for the fourth time on 27 September 1990 in the Queens Hall in Edinburgh, and agreed the package to be launched on St Andrews Day 1990.

It is generally agreed that the pace with which the Convention published its first attempt at consensus, taking barely six months, would have been slower if the Tories and SNP had taken their seats.[25] It was also recognised that the scheme launched in November 1992 was not complete. The remaining unanswered questions were:

- the detail of the electoral system

- the entrenchment of the Parliament to protect its existence against any future resentful Westminster government

- the future role of the job of Secretary of State for Scotland, and the number of Scottish MPs at Westminster post-home rule

- The representation of Scotland in the European Union[26]

With the exception of the issues outlined above, the remaining Ts and Is were crossed and dotted in the weeks between the Queens Hall meeting and the formal launch on 30 November at Glasgow's Royal Concert Hall.

The launch event began with a procession involving 50 of Scotland's 64 Council leaders. Declarations were signed, the Claim was reasserted, new commitments were sought and John Smith coined the memorable phrase that devolution was 'the settled will of the Scottish people.'[27] The launch event had to compete with the Scottish Green Party's announcement that it was quitting the Convention over the issue of a pre-legislative referendum. In 1995 the Scottish Green Party was welcomed back into the Convention.[28]

The launch of 'Towards Scotland's Parliament' did not mark the end of Convention deliberations. In March 1992 the Convention met to consider working party reports on electoral systems and parliamentary procedures. Statutory measures to ensure gender equality were vetoed by the Liberal Democrats while the question of procedures was referred to the parliament itself.[29] With the encouragement of the CSA, Bernard Crick and David Miller published their 'Crick/Miller' proposals on Standing Orders for the new parliament. During 1991/92, Jim Ross indulged in some freelance thinking on the creation of a class of constitutional provisions intended as an answer to the entrenchment question.[30]

Within days of the launch of 'Towards Scotland's Parliament', Prime Minister Margaret Thatcher was ousted with considerable impact on the Scottish political scene. Thatcher's ideology, style and persona were totally alien to majority Scottish opinion and she cut against the grain of the Scottish identity, culminating in the Poll Tax episode. As Tory Leader and Prime Minister Margaret Thatcher was more responsible than any other single individual for the increasing demand for Scottish constitutional change, and her departure had an impact on the tenor of debate in Scotland.

The above initiatives aside, the emphasis was on public campaigning in the months following November 1990. Harry Conroy's lines of reporting were somewhat complex. The CSA had raised Harry's salary, and he faithfully attended National Executive meetings, but he reported to the Convention's Campaign Co-ordinating Working Group, which included the senior aparatchiks of each of the Convention partners and set the direction of the campaign. The CSA was represented in that paramount council of the Convention by our convener Isobel Lindsay. The main objective of the campaign, which Harry was employed to direct, was to maximise media publicity for the Convention's proposal.

To that end a series of regional media launches featuring senior figures, were staged in the North of Scotland, the South West and Tayside. The Convention platform regularly consisted of Donald Dewar, Malcolm Bruce, Campbell Christie and Kenyon Wright. Conroy later estimated that Wright addressed an average of two public meetings per week during that period.[31]

Kenyon Wright's memorable sound bite, 'We say Yes', was reproduced on campaign materials for local campaigning, i.e. 100,000 tabloid newspapers and 100,000 leaflets. Supporters at large were asked to actively participate in the campaign by completing and returning 'We Say Yes!' postcards. A total of 5,000 cards were presented to the Scottish Office by Kenyon Wright and Isobel on 25 June 1991.

The campaign carried the attack to the enemy in a number of ways. On 6 February 1991, the Convention held a press conference for lobby journalists at the House of Commons. The Convention challenged Scottish Conservatives to a debate on the fringe of their own conference in May 1991.

Briefings were produced on different aspects of Scottish life, e.g. Education, Health and the Economy, outlining the difference that a Scottish Parliament could make. Briefings were also prepared for consulates and embassies.[32]

Lend Scotland Your Vote

The general election, finally called for 9 April 1992, was a long-time coming, Thatcher's successor, John Major, having taken the time to establish himself and bring the Gulf War to a victorious conclusion.

Throughout its existence the CSA had debated the pros and cons of encouraging tactical voting. The CSA had drawn back from issuing such a call at the 1987 election. The results of that election, however, demonstrated that if just 33,981 people, living in key constituencies, had cast their vote differently then no Conservative MPs would have been returned from Scottish constituencies. In 1992 there was a view that it would require a political shock of that magnitude to force a Tory Government, re-elected by England, to engage with the demand of the Scottish people for home rule.[33]

It was widely recognised, however, that such a tactic could threaten the cohesion of the home rule alliance and the CSA trod carefully in devising its initiative. It was decided to target the constituencies of three senior Conservatives: Michael Forsyth in Stirling, Ian Lang in Galloway and Lord James Douglas Hamilton in Edinburgh West. In each case, the CSA would urge the anti-Tory majority, on this one occasion, to lend their vote to Scotland by uniting behind the candidate of the party which had come second in 1987. The targeted trio were selected because their leading challengers belonged to different parties. Labour would replace Forsyth, the SNP would oust Lang and the Liberal Democrats would displace Lord James.[34]

Michael Forsyth's majority in 1987 was a very slender 548 votes and, as soon as the CSA campaign was announced, he sought immediate recourse from the courts. He argued that Section 75 of the Representation of the People's Act, 1983, prevented any person, or organisation, other than a candidate and his/her election agent, from approving expenditure deemed to be promoting one candidate over another.[35]

The CSA responded that our campaign would end before the declaration of the election, and Alan Lawson quipped that any meetings in the constituencies concerned would be held outdoors to prevent costs from being incurred.[36] Forsyth retorted that a legal ruling by Lord Ross, concerning elections to Lothian Regional Council, clarified that the prohibition in question applied from a time 'shortly before' the publication of the formal election timetable.[36]

Forsyth's persistence forced a tactical retreat. It was not a happy moment for the CSA. Despite the Campaign's genuine intention to ensure that the three pro-home rule parties would all gain from the initiative, Labour was concerned. Its constituency organisation in Edinburgh West claimed it was their candidate, not the Liberal Democrat, that was the main opposition to Lord James.[37]

. The tactical voting initiative caused anxieties for those of us in the CSA who were also active in our own political parties. This led to the tactical voting initiative falling on the shoulders of those who were not members of any party, or party members who were not currently active in their party.

Whatever concerns the CSA had about the stalled tactical voting initiative, they soon paled into insignificance as the results of the general election in Scotland became clear on the morning of Friday 10 April 1992.

NOTES AND REFERENCES

[1]   Kenyon Wright, *The People Say Yes!*, Argyll Publishing, 1997, pp.124/125
[2]   *Ibid*
[3]   CSA. Minutes of the National Executive Committee meeting, held on 22 November 1989
[4]   CSA. Minutes of the National Executive Committee meeting, held on 20 September 1989
[5]   CSA. Minutes of the National Executive Committee meeting, held on 22 November 1989
[6]   Andrew Marr, *The Battle for Scotland*, Penguin Books, London, 1992, p.206
[7]   CSA. Minutes of the Edinburgh Branch meeting held on 13 November 1989
[8]   CSA. Campaign News, December 1989
[9]   *Ibid*
[10] Andrew Marr, *The Battle for Scotland*, Penguin Books, London, 1992, p.208
[11] *Scotsman*, Friday 14 July 1989, p.4
[12] Scottish Liberal Democrat Leader, Malcolm Bruce, quoted in the *Glasgow Herald*, Monday 12 March 1990
[13] CSA. Minutes of the National Executive Committee meeting, May 1990

[14] CSA. Minutes of the National Executive Committee meeting, held on 22 August 1990

[15] *Scotsman,* 22 August 1990, p.4

[16] CSA. Minutes of the National Executive meeting, held on 25 July 1990

[17] *Ibid*

[18] Alan Armstrong in conversation with author, August 2000

[19] CSA. Minutes of the CSA National Executive Committee meeting, held on 19 September 1990

[20] Alan Armstrong in conversation with the author, August 2000

[21] See the *Scotsman,* 5 September 1990

[22] CSA. The Jim Boyack Memorial Project, Edinburgh, 1992, p.1 and p.23

[23] *Ibid*, pp.13-20

[24] *Ibid*, pp.9-10

[25] Donald Dewar quoted in the *Glasgow Herald* on Monday 24 September 1990, p.9

[26] *Scotsman*, Monday 24 September 1990, p.9

[27] Kenyon Wright, *The People Say Yes!*, Argyll Publishing, 1997, pp.139-143

[28] *Ibid*, p.139

[29] *Ibid*, pp.157-60

[30] *Ibid*, p.154

[31] Harry Conroy, 'Constitutional Convention Campaign', in Lindsay Paterson and David McCrone (editors), *The Scottish Government Yearbook 1992*, Unit for the Study of Government in Scotland, Edinburgh, 1992, p.82

[32] For an account of the Convention Campaign throughout 1991, see Harry Conroy in Lindsay Paterson and David McCrone (editors), *The Scottish Government Yearbook 1992*, pp.74-83

[33] *Glasgow Herald*, Wednesday 4 March 1992, p.3

[34] CSA. Press release, dated 3 March 1992

[35] *Glasgow Herald*, Wednesday 4 March 1992, p.1

[36] *Ibid*

[37] *Glasgow Herald*, Wednesday 4 March 1992, p.3

CHAPTER 6

Scotland's Parliament,
Scotland's Right

April 1992 to November 1995

The End of Scottish Politics?

In many ways the result of the general election of April 1992 was a repeat of the outcome of the 1987 contest. Labour remained dominant in Scotland while the British party of government, the Conservatives, were confined to a derisory rump. Rational assessments of the result were difficult to sustain, however, amid the massive wave of disappointment. Contrary to pre-election predictions, Labour had failed to oust the Conservatives in Britain as a whole while the Tories were perceived to have 'recovered' in Scotland by adding just 1% to their all time low performance in 1987. Elements of the Scottish media were central to this twisted perception of events. The Scottish Constitutional question had been the bread and butter of Scottish political reporting during the previous five years, and journalists and columnists feared they had lost their best story.[1] They blamed the situation on the Scottish electorate and the supposed lack of nerve that contributed to defeat in the 1979 referendum. One example of this journalistic hyperbole was Andrew Marr, now the BBC's UK Political Editor, who asked whether the 1992 result had marked 'the end of Scottish politics as a tale in its own right.'[2]

Media exaggeration aside, why did the predicted complete collapse of what remained of Scottish Conservatism fail to materialise in April 1992? As discussed earlier, the replacement of Margaret Thatcher with John Major had an impact on the tenor of Scottish attitudes to the Tories, and whatever his shortcomings, John Major was never the hate figure that Mrs Thatcher had been during her reign. The revolt against Mrs Thatcher's flagship policy, the Poll Tax, had its own impact on the Scottish electorate, which, in 1992, was 2% down on the number of people entitled to vote in 1987. Part of that drop may have been due to Poll Tax non-payers avoiding inclusion on the electoral register. It was also the case that the Tories tightly targeted their still considerable organisation on the seats they were defending. John Major launched a personal crusade to defend the Union from devolution, and the separation that he claimed would inevitably follow. Polling evidence suggests that Major's siren call mobilised English families living and working in Scotland. Among English-born electors in Scottish constituencies, the Tories averaged almost 30% while they scored less than 20% among Scottish-born electors.[3]

Reactions

The most startled reaction to the 1992 result came from the Liberal Democrats and their Leader, Malcolm Bruce. Bruce's majority in Gordon was much reduced on 1987, and those around him believed that their association with Labour in the Convention had lost them support in the rural constituencies of the North East.[4] In a reaction, described as the 'Gordon factor', leading Liberal Democrats called for a shift in emphasis to the federal reform of the United Kingdom as a whole. There were senior Lib-Dems, however, who rejected Bruce's response. David Steel, Joint Chair of the Convention, called for cross-party working to continue through the machinery of the Convention.[5]

The SNP retained the seats won in 1987 but lost Jim Sillars, the victor of Govan, and the gulf between their share of the vote and their opinion poll rating in late 1988/early '89 underlined the error they had made in shunning the Convention. Despite that lesson, Gordon Wilson and Sillars continued to oppose a conciliatory approach to the wider home rule movement while Alex Salmond supported contacts across party lines.[6]

There appeared to be natural allies on the maximalist home rule wing of the Labour Party, including MPs George Galloway, John

McAllion and Dennis Canavan, who founded Scotland United in the course of days following the election. The enthusiasm of Galloway and co. was counter-balanced by other Labour MPs, including Brian Wilson and Norman Hogg, who called for constitutional reform to be shifted to the back burner. In July 1992 Tom Clarke replaced Donald Dewar as Shadow Secretary of State for Scotland under John Smith, who had succeeded Neil Kinnock as UK Labour Leader.[7]

As far as the Conservatives were concerned, Michael Forsyth quit the Scottish Office for the Department of Employment. Lord Fraser of Carmylie was appointed as the Scottish Office Minister for constitutional affairs. He quickly moved to restore the Scottish Select Committee and launch the promised 'Taking Stock' investigation into Scotland's role in the Union.[8]

Go Forth and Multiply

Within forty eight hours of the declaration of the election result, no less than three new home rule campaign groups appeared. For a period of six months Scotland United demonstrated real dynamism and organised a series of rallies featuring top Scottish musicians including Ricky Ross and Deacon Blue, and Pat Kane of Hue and Cry.

On the day following the election, leading anti-nuclear campaigner Lorraine Mann called on people to join her in a vigil outside the old Royal High School, the intended site of the Scottish Parliament. It proved to be the origin of Democracy for Scotland, which maintained an impressive vigil for five years.

The other organisation established over that weekend was Common Cause, which was the outcome of a 'touchy feely' late night, all night gathering at the Church of Scotland's Carberry Towers retreat in East Lothian. Common Cause modelled itself on the Civic Forums, which played a leading role in the velvet revolutions of Eastern Europe, and demonstrated an intellectual ethos. Its leading figures included Church of Scotland minister Willie Storrar and critic, commentator and writer Joyce MacMillan.

A unifying feature of the new organisations was their challenge to John Major's claim to be a 'listening' Prime Minister by calling on him to hold a multi-option referendum on Scotland's constitutional future: the Status Quo, the Convention Scheme or Independence.[9]

So how did the CSA react to the formation of the new organisations? The CSA had never behaved in a propriertorial manner with regard to the home rule cause, and involvement in the CSA was not part of the conventional political career structure. Longstanding members of the CSA were influential in the new organisations. Isobel Lindsay, Moira Craig and Marion Ralls were leading lights in Common Cause while many Labour Party members, who were members of the CSA, were involved in Scotland United. Throughout the summer of 1992 it looked as though Scotland United might prove to be a bridge for a wider range of SNP supporters to cross party activity.

At the CSA Annual General Meeting held on 18 April 1992 Isobel Lindsay welcomed the new organisations:

> 'This is the way of Scottish politics – full of artificial divisions between parties which have ceased to be meaningful. Some people get on better with individuals from other parties than they do with those from their own. We have to find someway of getting round it.'[10]

At its delayed AGM the CSA joined in the call for a multi-option referendum.

Changes within the formal party political structure had a bearing on the fortunes of the home rule cause. Neil Kinnock shocked a shattered Labour Party by announcing his resignation, and a speedy selection process anointed the late John Smith as the new Labour leader. Smith's elevation created a domino effect of sorts. Smith recruited Scottish Labour Party Secretary, Murray Elder, to his London staff, Tom Clake succeeded Donald Dewar as Shadow Secretary of State for Scotland, and, to the surprise of many, Jack McConnell was appointed to the post left vacant by Murray Elder's departure.

Jack McConnell had strong home rule connections. As a teenager in Arran he had been a member of the SNP. At Stirling University he joined the Communist-influenced Broad Left, the CSA and the Labour Party. He was a founder member of Scottish Labour Action, argued for Labour's participation in the Constitutional Convention, and for a Scottish Parliament to be elected by a fair electoral system. These changes in the hierarchy of Scottish Labour, along with the replacement of the weary Malcolm Bruce by Jim Wallace as Scottish Liberal Democrat Leader, led to a revival of the Convention.[11]

Divisions in the CSA

June 1992 marked the end of Harry Conroy's tenure as the Constitutional Convention's Campaign Director. The CSA had enjoyed a close working relationship with Harry and as a momento the National Executive presented him with a piece of original artwork from the Jim Boyack Memorial Exhibition.[12] In October the National Executive of the CSA approved the long anticipated name change and agreed to recommend a constitutional amendment to become the Campaign for a Scottish Parliament (CSP).[13]

Name change aside, much thinking was underway during the summer of 1992 as to the future of the home rule campaign and the Constitutional Convention. Alan Lawson took the view that the Convention had fulfilled its role and that it was time for a new initiative, a 'Shadow' or 'Alternative' Parliament. It was proposed that this forum, composed of Scotland's elected representatives, would meet regularly to debate government policy and propose alternatives, thereby illustrating how a Scottish Parliament would work.[14] The proposal was opposed by Isobel Lindsay. She argued that it smacked too much of a 'breakaway' for the taste of a Labour Party which now had several Scots – Smith, Brown, Cook, Dewar – among its UK Leadership. If the initiative was launched and failed, the CSP's credibility would be undermined.[15]

Alan believed that Isobel's opposition stemmed from her desire to keep the Convention centre-stage as she was a major player within it. He also took the view that while Isobel was a considerable thinker, she often failed to consider how ideas were translated into action, and it was Brian Duncan, Alan Milnes and himself who had to fill in the detail. There were concerns that Isobel, as Convener, had a tendency to commit the CSP to positions and initiatives without due reference to the National Executive.[16] Isobel believed that Alan regarded her as the major obstacle to his own ideas on the way forward, and that their 'tactical disagreement became very personal.'[17]

Matters came to a head at the National Executive Committee meeting held on 18 November 1992 when a motion of no confidence in Isobel was tabled by Alan Lawson, Alan Milnes and Brian Duncan. It was defeated by a margin of six votes to four. I was present at the meeting and abstained. It may have been a 'wimpish' course of action but I did not believe that the 'no confidence' was justified, but I held the two Alans and Brian in too high a regard to vote 'against them'. Ten days later, the trio announced their resignation from the CSP National Executive in an open letter to its members. As would have been expected of them, they post-dated their resignations to 31 December, to ensure a tidy hand over to new office bearers, and to complete the task of closing the CSP Office in Edinburgh, as previously agreed by the Executive.[18]

The CSP Executive met on 15 December to discuss the stewardship of the organisation until the next scheduled Annual General Meeting on 20 March 1993. Douglas Chalmers of the Democratic Left (formerly the Communist Party of Great Britain) took over as acting-Secretary, assisted by Liberal Democrat Marion Ralls who took over as Secretary on a permanent basis.[19]

Isobel's role at the centre of the divisions of late 1992 may well have played a part in her deciding to step down as Convener in 1993 to be succeeded by Moira Craig.

Moira Craig

Psychologist Moira Craig studied at the University of Glasgow and chaired the University's Labour Club at a time when its ranks included the likes of John Smith and Donald Dewar. In the early 1980s Moira joined the Social Democratic Party, and although she supported the subsequent Liberal Democrat merger, she has never considered herself as a 'Liberal', and would never have joined the old Liberal Party. She was, however, firmly attached to one particular traditional strand in Old Liberal thinking, home rule for Scotland.

That enthusiasm led to her becoming the CSA/P's last National Convener. She steered the Campaign from 1993 to its dissolution in 1999, and she represented it in the Constitutional Convention.

Between 1983 and 2001, Moira flew the SDP/Alliance/Liberal Democrat banner in no less than four council elections, four general elections and one Scottish election. Within the Liberal Democrats Scottish structure she held the post of Vice Convener. Given her service to the Lib Dem cause, it came as something of a surprise to learn that she had resigned her membership of the party. It was an expression of her frustration with the constraints of the party system, which many in and around the CSA/P hoped would be loosened in our new political disposition. Margo MacDonald, Dennis Canavan and hospital campaigner Dr Jean Turner aside, parties still rule at Holyrood.

Alan Lawson

Dundonian Alan Lawson trained in computing and spent 1975/76 in Zambia setting up computer systems for the copper mining industry. He joined the SNP in 1982 and remained a member until 1984.[20] A founding member of the CSA/P, Alan was involved in early initiatives, such as the Festival of the People in 1980, and the campaign against the Royal Bank of Scotland merger in 1981. Alan stepped up his involvement in 1984 when he went freelance in order to devote more time to the Radical Scotland magazine and the CSA/P. For eight years, until his breach with Isobel, he was at the centre of CSA/P activity.

It was Alan's idea to set up the Constitutional Steering Committee as a way of jump starting the Constitutional Convention, and he was involved in the exhaustive round of meetings and discussion, from July 1988 to March 1989, that led to its establishment. It is his proudest political claim and he firmly believes that those nine months were the CSA/CSP's greatest hour.[21]

Alan has a tough political skin and does not suffer fools gladly, attributes which are essential in sustaining lengthy periods of self-sacrificing political activism. Alan had been among those who had had lobbied for Alan Armstrong to take over as Convener, believing it to be in the interests of the CSA at that moment. When Jim Boyack died in 1990 it was Alan who acted to ensure that Jim's contribution to the home rule movement was recognised. The following year, it was Alan Lawson who initiated and managed the Jim Boyack Memorial Project on behalf of the CSA.

The circumstances of the breach between Isobel and Alan have already been discussed. I am of the view, however, that political 'burn-out' had much to do with it. Alan had in essence been a full time home rule campaigner since 1984. In the summer of 1992, we all faced at least another four or five years campaigning before there was any likely prospect of achieving our goal.

Euro Summitry and the Coalition for Scottish Democracy

Welcome distraction from internal wrangles was provided by the European Council Heads of Government meeting held in Edinburgh over the second weekend in December 1992. Scotland's opposition parties and all of the home rule pressure groups were involved in organising a massive demonstration under the slogan 'Scotland Demands Democracy'. An estimated 30,000 people rallied on Edinburgh's Meadows, making it the largest Scottish political demonstration of modern times.[22]

The event was an outstanding public success but, behind the scenes, there was the usual party wrangling. Henry McLeish, the senior figure on the platform deputising for a convalescing Tom Clarke, was barracked by a section of the crowd. Given the great success of the Euro demonstration, and the tensions between the political parties involved, the CSP was among those calling for a co-ordinating structure involving the organisations that had taken part in Euro demonstration, with the exception of the political parties. Accordingly, the civic organisations involved established the Coalition for Scottish Democracy in March 1993. It was chaired by Campbell Christie and serviced by the STUC.[23]

Taking Stock

While Scotland's civic organisations were coming together in the Coalition for Scottish Democracy, the opposition parties were involved in trilateral talks of their own in an attempt to arrive at a common response to the Tories' 'Taking Stock' exercise, which would be published under the title of 'Scotland in the Union'.[24] As a reply to the demand for home rule, the exercise was totally inadequate. It sought to resolve the Scottish question as if it were simply a matter of symbols and form. While such things are not unimportant, the government ignored the more material aspirations which blended with constitutional change to produce the heady home rule brew.[25]

If the Tories failed to understand the basis of the demand for home rule, the SNP failed to appreciate the potency of the 'Tartan Tory' jibe in the Labour-supporting areas of Scotland. In March 1993, the Labour Party pounced upon SNP support for the government over a detail of the Maastricht debate on the future of the European Union. Labour cited the SNP's siding with the Tories as a reason for breaking with the trilateral process. While Labour exaggerated the significance of the SNP's support on a technical detail, the Nationalists' actions demonstrated their failure to appreciate just how emotive the charge of collaborating with the Tories could be.[26]

The major results of 'Scotland in the Union' were a higher profile for the Scottish Grand Committee, the transfer of a couple of responsibilities from Whitehall to the Scottish Office and greater branding of the Scottish Office and its work.[27]

Out of the Impasse

In April 1993, a full year after the general election, the Constitutional Convention agreed a fresh initiative. The Scottish Constitutional Commission was established to revisit the major issues that had been glossed over in 'Towards Scotland's Parliament' and to make recommendations to the Convention.[28] The key issues were:

1   Proposals for elections to, and representation in, a Scottish Parliament, including electoral systems and gender balance.

2   The Constitutional implications, at United Kingdom and local government level, of the establishment of a Scottish Parliament.

The Commission's Joint Chairs were Joyce McMillan and the late John Pollock, former General Secretary of the Educational Institute for Scotland and Labour grandee. Unfortunately, John Pollock resigned over an administrative wrangle before the work of the Commission got underway. As with the Convention, the Commission was serviced by COSLA. Bruce Black continued as Secretary until his retirement in April 1994, at which point he was replaced by Liz Manson.[29]

The Constitutional Commission did not report until October 1994, and in the intervening year the CSP continued with campaigning initiatives. On 14 December 1993 the CSP was represented by Isobel Lindsay on a Coalition for Scottish Democracy delegation to the European Union. Led by Campbell Christie, the delegation presented a petition to the President of the European Parliament, Egon Klepsch, in Strasbourg. The petition, signed by the leaders of Scotland's home rule parties, asserted the right of the Scottish people to self-determination, and called for a multi-option referendum to settle Scotland's constitutional future.[30]

The main focus for CSP activists in late 1993 was the Falkirk Referendum. Organised under the banner of the Coalition for Scottish Democracy, this mini-referendum was designed to illustrate that such an exercise could be carried out nation wide without the sanction or support of the state.

28,000 ballot papers were delivered by hand to electors residing in ten electoral wards over a two day period, 4 and 5 December 1993.[31] The ballot paper asked:

Are you in favour of the establishment of an elected Scottish Parliament?

It continued:

If a Scottish Parliament were established, would you wish it to be:

A   Within the UK

Or

B   Independent of the UK[32]

Completed ballots were collected up to Sunday 12 December, and the result was counted and announced on Monday 13 December.

The Falkirk Referendum was a gamble for both the CSD and the CSP. Prior to the referendum, Campbell Christie had stated that a 35% response rate would be credible, given the turnout in local government elections.[33] The best efforts of CSP members and others managed to collect 7,788 papers, a 28% turnout. Of those who voted, 88% were in favour of establishing a Scottish Parliament, with 12% against. 54% were in favour of remaining within the UK, while 46% supported independence.[34]

The *Scotsman* proclaimed 'Poor Turn Out', while Scottish Tory Chairman, Michael Hirst described it as 'a stunning belly flop.' Objectively, the support for a Parliament, and for independence, was way ahead of regular opinion poll results. Isobel Lindsay sought to explain the result, admitting that those who participated were among the most committed to home rule.[35] One bonus from the Falkirk campaign was the involvement of Bill Hendry, who subsequently joined the CSP National Executive and served the Campaign well during its remaining years.

What had been another frustrating year for the CSP ended on something of a high note. On 30 December the Court of Session upheld an appeal by Grampian Regional Council against a ruling by the Controller of Audit, supported by the Commission of Local Authority Accounts, that financial contributions to the Convention, via the CSP, were against the law. The Court of Session ruled that the creation, or not, of a Scottish Parliament was connected with the interests of the Council and its inhabitants. Given that the Convention was open to all, support for the Convention could not be regarded as advocating support for one political party over another.[36]

From Scottish Senate to Scottish Civic Assembly

In the debate between Isobel Lindsay and Alan Lawson, which resulted in the latter's resignation from the CSP Executive, Isobel had alluded to the possibilities of Scottish civic organisations coming together to debate issues facing different sectors of Scottish life.

Solutions to problems could be suggested and referred for consideration to the Scottish Parliament once it was established. Isobel had originally floated this concept as a more practical alternative to Alan's proposal for a Shadow Parliament. Throughout 1993, however, she and others continued to work on the idea.

In January 1994 Marion Ralls, who by that time had become National Secretary, presented a paper on 'General Campaign Objectives' to the CSP National Executive. She argued that a 'Scottish Senate', not full of elected politicians, but including representatives from 'key sectors' of Scottish life, e.g. business, law, arts, agriculture, education etc. could act as a credible voice for Scotland in the immediate future. Post home rule it could continue to have a role, inputing to, and commenting on, legislation before the Scottish Parliament. Marion also argued that such a model could inform the wider debate on a second chamber to replace the House of Lords at Westminster.[37] The CSP National Executive endorsed the paper and agreed that it should be raised with the Coalition for Scottish Democracy.

The proposal was presented to the Coalition in February 1994, and it was agreed to call a consultative conference in June 1994.[38] Speaking to *Scotland on Sunday* prior to the Consultative Conference, Campbell Christie, in his capacity as Chair of the Coalition, described the Senate proposal as follows:

'The idea is to get civic society in Scotland used to developing policies in the areas that government influences – justice, health, education and transport – and to build public awareness of what could be done in a Scottish Parliament.'[39]

On Saturday 18 June 1994, more than two hundred delegates assembled at the old Royal High School on Calton Hill for the 'Consultative Conference on the Establishment of a Scottish Senate'. The major disappointment was the absence of any meaningful representation from the business community. Although political parties were not represented as such, the SNP declined to welcome the initiative, and Labour and the Liberal Democrats were tentative in their support.

The main debate at the Consultative Conference was over the title 'Senate'. Back in the 1970s/early 80s, the term had been applied to a non-elected body proposed by some Conservatives as an alternative to a Scottish Parliament, and was therefore unpopular. There were also those concerned that they were being asked to endorse the notion that the Scottish Parliament should have a second chamber, and the term 'Senate' underlined that concern. It was therefore agreed to change the title to the Scottish Civic Assembly.[40] It was initially serviced by the Coalition for Scottish Democracy and later by the Scottish Council for Voluntary Organisations.

The Scottish Civic Assembly continues today, in the guise of the Scottish Civic Forum, an important sounding board in home rule Scotland. Interestingly, a similar forum is part of the Belfast (Good Friday) Agreement for bringing lasting peace and democracy to Northern Ireland.

With Regret

It was with regret that the CSP learned of the resignation of Greg McCarra in July 1994. Greg was a founder member of the CSA/P, had served as press officer for a number of years and played a leading role in the early work on the Constitutional Convention. Following the resignation of Alan Armstrong, Greg had been the most prominent SNP figure to remain active within the CSP. In his resignation letter, Greg stated that his support for home rule was strictly evolutionary, as he believed that the establishment of a Scottish Parliament within the UK would eventually lead to independence. He argued that the CSP had abandoned the commitment to the sovereignty of the Scottish people, as outlined in the Claim, was thirled to Labour's devolution proposals and would be likely to campaign against independence if a multi option referendum was ever held.

In reply, National Secretary, Marion Ralls, argued that Greg was underestimating the number of evolutionists within the ranks of the CSP and, faced with a multi-option referendum, the CSP would seek to maintain maximum unity around the principle of constitutional change but would not take a stance on home rule versus independence.[41] Greg remained unconvinced.

The Commision Reports

On the evening of 10 August 1994, the CSP National Executive met with Joyce MacMillan, Chair of the Constitutional Commission appointed by the Convention in April 1993 to report back on some of the more difficult questions facing it. Correctly, Joyce did not provide the CSP with an exclusive leak as to what the Commission would recommend when it reported in the autumn. Instead she provided us with an idea of how the Commission was going about its work.[42]

The Constitutional Commission report 'Further Steps Towards a Scheme for Scotland's Parliament' was launched at a press conference in Edinburgh on 25 October 1994, some eighteen months after it was established. There were a few disappointments. The report was divided into three sections.

1   With regard to the electoral system, the Commission recommended the Additional Member Scheme. On the detail of the system, they recommended a parliament with seventy two members elected from constituencies by first-past-the-post, with five additional members elected from each of eight regional lists, thereby creating a parliament of 112 members. The report failed to make it absolutely clear whether or not the additional members would be 'corrective.' i.e. allocated to reduce the non-proportional results in the constituencies. Media coverage of the report concentrated on this confusion.[43]

2   On the question of gender balance, the Commission rejected what it described as 'manipulation' of the electoral system. Instead it called on political parties to ensure that by the second term of a Scottish Parliament at least 40% of their Members of the Scottish Parliament (MSPs) would be women.

3   On the wider constitutional implications of Scottish home rule, the Commission proposed retaining seventy two Scottish MPs at Westminster, until the anomaly of Scotland's over-

representation could be dealt with by the development of regional government in England or by a boundary commission review. The report suggested that the post of Secretary of State for Scotland should be retained for a transitional period. On the question of entrenching a Scottish Parliament, the Commission joined with those that argued that this could not be achieved in a political system based on the absolute sovereignty of Westminster, but added that political and moral entrenchment were every bit as effective as legal entrenchment.[44]

The CSP's autumn conference took place in Stirling's Golden Lion Hotel on Saturday 29 October, providing CSP members with an early opportunity to discuss the Commission's Report, which had been issued earlier that week. The main area of concern was the recommended ratio of additional members to constituency members. The CSP supported fair elections and even if all additional members were allocated correctively in each region it would not be enough to achieve a fair result overall. There was support for the proposal to phase out the post of Secretary of State for Scotland, but the Commission's recommendations on gender, Scottish MPs at Westminster and entrenchment added little or nothing to the debate. The overall view of the CSP members present was that the Constitution Commission had been a missed opportunity.[45]

The Scottish Constitutional Convention met for the eleventh time on Friday 2 December 1994 to receive the report of the Commission. A positive gloss was put upon what had been achieved, but in reality the Commission passed the political hot potatoes back to the Convention. The Convention also approved the 'Preparing for Change Project', aimed at informing different sections of Scottish society about what home rule could mean for them. Esther Roberton was appointed as the Programme Co-ordinator.

Campaigners' Pack

More positively, the CSP autumn conference saw the launch of the CSP Campaigners' Pack. In July 1994 the CSP National Executive had agreed to create a loose-leaf folder containing inserts on the key issues facing the home rule movement, which I was asked to produce and edit. It began with an attractive folder and an initial insert on the history of the home rule question. Over the next three years a further twenty inserts were added. New members received a full pack on joining, while existing members received new inserts as they were produced. The Pack provided CSP members with the information and briefing required to enable them to act as informed advocates of the case for home rule.

The CSP concluded the campaigning year with a St Andrews Day Social celebrating the contribution of New Scots to our national life.

Hands Across the Borders

In early 1995 the CSP organised an important event designed to share information among democracy campaigners throughout the British Isles. 'Hands Across the Borders' was held at Winton Lodge near Biggar over the weekend of 10-12 February.

The impressive line up of speakers included Lord Richard Holme, the Liberal Democrats senior UK spokesperson on constitutional reform, George Robertson, the Shadow Secretary of State for Scotland, Campbell Christie, John Tomeney from the Campaign for a Northern (English) Assembly, Tom Nairn, writer and academic, and John Osmond of the Campaign for a Welsh Assembly. The conference was chaired by Isobel Lindsay.

Labour Thinks Again

Where the Constitutional Commission feared to tread, Scottish Labour sought to lead, and the party's Scottish Executive went to its annual conference in March 1995 to seek authority to advance bilateral discussion with the Liberal Democrats on the question of gender balance in a Scottish Parliament. The statement argued that the Parliament should be elected by AMS, that the Parliament should be large enough to facilitate positive action and that the two parties should commit themselves to selecting an equal number of men and women.[46]

On 31 May 1995, Tommy Sheppard, Scottish Labour's Assistant General Secretary, wrote to local parties and affiliates asking them to return their views, by 18 August, on the number of members that should sit in a Scottish Parliament.[47] Labour's 1979 devolution proposals envisaged an Assembly with 144 members. In 1995, concerns over the number of backbenchers compared with Executive Members, international comparisons and the scope to operate positive action led responding organisations to endorse 144. Labour's Scottish Executive seemed set to endorse that figure at a meeting on 9 September. On 7 September 1995, however, George Robertson, Labour's Shadow Scottish Secretary, and Lib Dem leader, Jim Wallace, issued a joint statement endorsing a parliament of 129 members. Their action created a lot of political froth as it pre-empted an internal Labour consultation exercise and was presented to the Convention as a fait accompli.

In his book, *The People Say Yes!*, Kenyon Wright acknowledges that the two leaders had 'acted in a way that by passed our normal democratic structures.'[48] He goes on to claim that he had urged them to act in the manner they did in order to break a deadlock in the Convention. The reality was that the Labour leadership wanted a 'small' Parliament, but its own consultation supported 144. Robertson used Wright and Wallace to pre-empt Labour's consultation. Seven years on, it may seem to be an argument about nothing, but a parliament of 144, 72 constituency members and 72 additional members, would have produced fully proportional election results.

By the summer of 1995, John Smith had been dead for a year, and, under Tony Blair, Labour re-visited a couple of commitments contained in the 1992 'Towards Scotland's Parliament'. Labour was now of the view that any suggestion of entrenchment should not be included in the legislation establishing a Scottish Parliament. Instead, Westminster would approve a declaration to the effect that the Scottish Parliament could not be abolished, nor radically changed, without the support of the Scottish people. At that point, in the summer of 1995, some Conventioneers, including CSP activists, suggested that we should seek political and moral entrenchment by making the establishing legislation subject to a referendum of the Scottish people. The major players dismissed the idea.[49]

The other issue for consideration was the central question of how a home rule Scotland would be financed. In 'Towards Scotland's Parliament', the Convention agreed a system of assigned revenues whereby all income tax and VAT collected in Scotland would stay in Scotland, and the remainder of Scotland's income would come from the Treasury as part of an equalisation exercise. The CSP, through our Convention Co-ordinating Committee representative, Isobel Lindsay, supported the assigned revenues formula as a compromise between a block grant and the Parliament having some control over its income guaranteed.

Kenyon Wright has claimed that in the summer of 1995 Labour persuaded its Convention partners that the system they had endorsed in 1992 was unwieldy and unworkable.[50] The CSP heard it differently. Marion Ralls, as National Secretary, was deputising for Isobel at a meeting of the Convention Co-ordinating Committee when it was told by Jack McConnell: 'you're not having that'. Marion recollects the incident very clearly as McConnell's approach was so contrary to the ethos the Convention was supposedly encouraging.[51] There are those who agree with Wright that it was a fuss over nothing as the 1995 revision in no way reduced the amount that Scotland would receive, nor the right of the Parliament to alter the basic rates of income tax, within agreed parameters. The significance of the assigned revenues debate, however, was that it represented a retreat on Scotland's revenue rights.

With Labour's requested revisions agreed, the second Constitutional Convention scheme for Scottish home rule, 'Scotland's Parliament, Scotland's Right', was approved by a full meeting of the Convention held on 20 October 1995 at the former Royal High School. The scheme was launched on St Andrews Day, 30 November 1995, in the Church of Scotland Assembly Hall on the Mound, almost six and a half years after the inaugural meeting of the Convention, in that same venue, on 31 March 1989. Matters had come full circle, or so it seemed.

NOTES AND REFERENCES

1   Ian McWhirter, 'The Disaster that Never Was, The Failure of Scottish Opposition After the 1992 General Election', in Lindsay Paterson (editor) *Scottish Affairs* No.1, Autumn 1992, p.4

2   Andrew Marr, *The Battle for Scotland*, Penguin, London, 1992, p.211

3   For further detail on the 1992 general election, see Christopher Harvie, *Scotland and Nationalism: Scottish Society and Nationalism: Society and Politics* (Third Edition), Routledge, London, 1998, p.238

4   Kenyon Wright, *The People Say Yes!*, Argyll Publishing, 1997, pp.170/171

5   Peter Lynch, 'The Scottish Constitutional Convention 1992-1995' in *Scottish Affairs*, No.15, Spring 1996, Unit for the Government of Scotland, Edinburgh, p.6

6   Iain McWhirter, 'The Disaster that Never Was, The Failure of Scottish Opposition After the 1992 General Election', in Lindsay Paterson (editor) *Scottish Affairs*, No.1, Autumn 1992, p.6

7   *Ibid*, p.5

8   *Ibid*, p.6

9   CSA. Minutes of the Annual General Meeting, held on Saturday 18 April 1992

10 *Glasgow Herald*, Saturday 18 April, 1992, p.3

11 Kenyon Wright, *The People Say Yes!*, Argyll publishing, 1997, pp.170/171

12 CSA. Minutes of the National Executive Committee meeting, held on 17 June 1992

13 CSA. Minutes of National Executive Committee meeting, held on 28 October 1992

14 Alan Lawson in conversation with the author, August 2000

15 Correspondence with Isobel Lindsay, August 2000

16 Alan Lawson in conversation with the author, August 2000

17 Correspondence with Isobel Lindsay, August 2000

18 Letter of resignation from Brian Duncan, Alan Lawson and Alan Milnes, dated 28 November 1992

19 CSP. National Executive Committee Extraordinary meeting, held on 15 December 1992

20 Alan Lawson in conversation with the author, August 2000

21 *Ibid*

22 Kenyon Wright, *The People Say Yes!*, Argyll Publishing, 1997, pp.175/176

23 CSP. *Campaign*, 'Campaign for a Scottish Parliament' Issue 2, June 1993

24 Peter Lynch, 'The Scottish Constitutional Convention 1992-1995' in

   Scottish Affairs, No.15, Spring 1996, Unit for the Government of Scotland, Edinburgh, pp.1-16

[25] *Ibid*

[26] Lindsay Paterson, 'The Failure of Scotland's Political Parties' in Lindsay Paterson (editor) *Scottish Affairs*, No.3, Spring 1993, p.3

[27] Statement by the Secretary of State for Scotland, Tuesday 9 March 1993, JSS00308.033

[28] Peter Lynch, 'The Scottish Constitutional Convention 1992-1995' *in Scottish Affairs*, No.15, Spring 1996, Unit for the Government of Scotland, Edinburgh, p.6

[29] Kenyon Wright, *The People Say Yes!*, Argyll Publishing, 1997, pp.179-183

[30] *Glasgow Herald*, Saturday 11 December 1993, p.3

[31] *Glasgow Herald*, Monday 13 December 1993, p.7

[32] CSP. Paper on the Falkirk referendum

[33] *Glasgow Herald*, Monday 13 December, 1993, p.7

[34] *Scotsman*, Tuesday 14 December 1993, p.1

[35] *Ibid*. p.3

[36] Kenyon Wright, *The People Say Yes!*, Argyll publishing, 1997, pp.193-194

[37] CSP. General Objectives, January 1994

[38] Coalition for Scottish Democracy, The Scottish Senate

[39] *Scotland on Sunday*, 5 June 1994, p.3

[40] *Scotland on Sunday*, 19 June 1994, p.3

[41] Marion Ralls to Greg McCarra, dated 12 July 1994

[42] CSP. Minutes of the Extraordinary National Executive, held on 10 August 1994

[43] *Herald*, Wednesday 26 October 1994, p.4

[44] Kenyon Wright, *The People Say Yes!*, Argyll Publishing, 1997, pp.197-201

[45] CSP. Minutes of the Autumn Conference, held in the Golden Lion Hotel, Stirling, on 29 October 1994

[46] 'Scottish Parliament – Gender Representation', Supplementary Report to the 80th Conference of the Scottish Labour Party, Scottish Labour Party, Glasgow, 1995

[47] Scottish Labour Party, Scottish Parliament-Further development of Policy, Glasgow, dated 31 May 1995

[48] Kenyon Wright, *The People Say Yes!*, Argyll Publishing, 1997, pp.213

[49] Moira Craig in conversation with the author, August 2000

[50] Kenyon Wright, *The People Say Yes!*, Argyll Publishing, 1997, pp.218/219

[51] Marion Ralls in conversation with the author, June 2000

CHAPTER 7

Scotland Forward

1996 to 1999

London Wakes Up

While Labour, under its new Leader Tony Blair, had demanded a couple of changes to the Convention scheme in the summer of 1995, New Labour UK was not finished with revisions. Scottish home rule came under the scrutiny of Labour's Irvine Committee, a high powered group chaired by Lord Derry Irvine, to scrutinise manifesto commitments on aspects of constitutional reform. Tony Blair's Shadow Cabinet, in the main, did not come from the generation of Labour parliamentarians who sat through exhausting marathon Commons' sittings as the Callaghan Government legislated for a Scottish Assembly. Many did not appreciate the magnitude of the legislative challenge, until the Irvine Committee reported to the Shadow Cabinet seminars held at Oxford's Templeton Management College in the Spring of 1996.

There were fears that in government, Labour backbenchers and Lords might baulk when they realised the time and effort required to legislate for devolution. Would it be better to pre-empt possible political problems, and short circuit the process, by staging a pre-legislative referendum in the first months of a new Labour Government?[1]

Throughout May 1996 the London media carried stories that Labour was set to ditch the Convention's policy of empowering a Scottish Parliament to vary the basic rate of income tax in Scotland within limited parameters. According to journalists, Labour, with fresh memories of how the issue of taxation had played in 1992, was concerned that debate on the 'Tartan Tax' in Scotland might be a factor in England come the general election. But the media failed to grasp that it was simply not credible in Scotland to dump the commitment.[2]

Better to insulate the rest of the UK by making the tax varying power subject to a specific second question in the proposed referendum, and by making it very clear that a Scottish Labour Administration in Edinburgh would not exercise that power during the Scottish Parliament's first term. It is not the purpose of this monograph to add to what has been written about the decision to insist on a pre-legislative referendum, but it is only right that I explain the reaction of the CSP, its members and the other Scottish home rule groups.

On 24 June 1996 a meeting was held in the House of Commons. It involved Tory Blair, his deputy John Prescott, George Robertson, Shadow Secretary of State for Scotland, Ann Taylor, Shadow Leader of the Commons, Jack Straw, Shadow Home Secretary, and Donald Dewar, Robin Cook and Gordon Brown, Scotland's senior Labour MPs.[3] Those present either agreed, or were told, that the Party's pre-manifesto process, 'The Road to the Manifesto', would commit an incoming Labour Government to a two question referendum on the establishment of a Scottish Parliament, and its ability to vary income tax. Talking about that meeting some three years later, Donald Dewar told the BBC's Brian Taylor that:

'All I would say was that I think Tony had a big influence.'[4]

It was agreed that Jack McConnell should be summoned to London on 25 June to be brought into the loop.[5] The 26th would be devoted to briefing key people, and George Robertson would front a public announcement in Glasgow on 27 June. This political choreography was wrong footed when the details of the referendum appeared in the *Independent* newspaper on 25 June.

The failure to notify and consult played badly. John McAllion, responsible for devolution on Labour's Shadow Scottish frontbench, learned about events as he travelled to Westminster on the morning of 26 June. He met Jim Wallace, who had been informed of events by Paddy Ashdown on the evening of the 24th.[6] Insult was added to injury by the fact that the Constitutional Convention Executive had met on 24 June, and conducted its business unaware of the massive change of strategy that was about to be imposed upon it.

David Steel was particularly angry as he and George Robertson had journeyed to London together, without Robertson taking the opportunity to warn him of what was coming. Lord Harry Ewing, Steel's co-chair of the Convention, resigned in protest and John McAllion resigned from his frontbench position.[7] On the 26th the STUC had been told by George Robertson that media reports about a referendum were inaccurate.[8]

On 28 June Tony Blair came to Scotland and among those he met with was Kenyon Wright, in his capacity as Chair of the Constitutional Convention's Executive. Blair committed himself to the Convention scheme, and to delivering it within a year.[9]

Concerns persisted and the referendum decision, or the manner of its taking, created worries about the way that London had intervened and what that intervention meant for the future workings of devolution. There was also a view that the second question was an open invitation to the Scottish people to reject that particular component of the Convention scheme.

Guerilla warfare continued in the Labour Party throughout the summer of 1996 but by early September the Leadership finally had its way as both sides of the argument collapsed in exhaustion.

In Convention terms, the debate came to a head on 26 July 1996. Faced with Jim Wallace, David Steel, Campbell Christie, and Moira Craig representing the CSP, George Robertson and Jack McConnell found themselves outnumbered. Despite the arithmetic, however, there could only be one outcome. The guarantees given by Blair to Kenyon Wright on 28 June were underlined.[10]

Carry on Campaigning

The problems created by the referendum row distracted home rule activists from concentrating on advocating the case for a Scottish Parliament. Prior to the referendum debacle there were concerns in the CSP that the Convention had failed to publish a popular guide to home rule and the Convention scheme. Frustrated by the delay the CSP decided to invest its own funds in the production of such a publication. In April 1996 we published the first edition of *The Blue*

Print for Scotland, an A4, four page, full colour brochure. The title recalled the *Blue Print* published in the late 1940s by the Covenant movement, and a document produced by the CSA in the early 1980s. It proved to be a popular, well received publication and the initial print run was the first in a number of editions produced over the course of the next eighteen months.

In the Spring of 1996 the CSP took its first steps along the virtual highway with the launch of a website: edin.easynet.co.uk/cscoparl/. One of those involved was Mark Loftus, who, along with colleague Andrew Burns, provided an active link between the work of the CSP and Charter 88. One example of that co-operation was a programme of joint CSP/Charter 88 meetings in Edinburgh and Glasgow during 1995 and 1996.[11] The Annual General Meeting of the CSP in April 1996 re-elected Moira Craig as Convener, Marion Ralls as National Secretary and Isobel Lindsay, Eric Canning and myself as Vice Conveners. We were joined by Duncan Clark in the role of Treasurer, and this was the group of officers who steered the CSP through the final years of its existence.[12]

Back on the campaign trail, the CSP took the message of home rule into Scotland's secondary schools with a competition launched in the autumn of 1996. It asked young Scots to draw up a job description for a Member of the Scottish Parliament (MSP). It was designed to get young people thinking about the varied roles and functions of a member of a Scottish legislature. The prize for the best individual essay was £100 while collective projects could win an AppleMac computer for their school.[13]

Partners for a Parliament

The key issue arising from the decision to call a pre-legislative referendum on a Scottish Parliament was how the pro-home rule YES campaign should be organised. Tony Blair had confirmed that an incoming Labour Government would support a broad-based campaign. For those of us haunted by memories of 1979 this was a central issue. To be perfectly honest it was unlikely that any of the existing home rule pressure groups had the resources or credibility to act as an umbrella for the others. Any organisation capable of embracing the spectrum of pro-home rule opinion could not afford any political baggage. It pointed to the creation of a new organisation.

In early October 1996 I was asked to join Moira Craig and Isobel Lindsay at a meeting in Isobel's office at Strathclyde University. We were joined by Nigel Smith. I knew Nigel from the CSA/CSP and he had supported the various business initiatives we had attempted across the years. He informed us that he was gathering funds to commission opinion polling on public attitudes towards a Scottish Parliament. He intended that the results from the polling should inform the strategy for a home rule alliance which, at that time, he was calling 'Partners for a Parliament'. Nigel raised the necessary cash from trade unions, including the EIS, and the Rowantree Reform Trust. The results of the polling were analysed by the BBC's Peter Kellner. The greatest degree of agreement was around the following statements:

'It is time that important decisions affecting Scotland were made by a Scottish Parliament elected by the Scottish people rather than hundreds of miles away in London.'

'Scotland needs to take more control over its own destiny and stop blaming other people for its problems.'

The polling also revealed that as many as 30% of Conservative voters favoured the creation of a Scottish Parliament. It also detected concern over the tax varying power.[14]

On 24 January 1997 the Executive Committee of the Scottish Constitutional Convention agreed to entrust its remit, to mobilise support for its scheme, to 'Partners for a Parliament'.[15]

Having sounded out all of the key players confidentially, little more could be achieved before the coming general election.

Nigel Smith

Managing Director of David Auld Valves Ltd., Nigel Smith spent much of his early career organising, closing and establishing engineering plants and commissioning new products. He had been a respected member of various organisations, including the Scottish Engineering Employers' Association (1985-90), the Broadcasting Council for Scotland (1986-90) and the Glasgow Development Agency's Strategy Review Panel (1993-94). One of the leading home rulers in the business community, he had presented the business case for devolution at a high powered conference organised by *The Herald* and the BBC's Today programme in April 1996.[16]

Following the decision on the referendum in the summer of 1996, Nigel had methodically worked his way around key Labour figures and persuaded them of his 'bona fides'. Nigel also had a degree of credibility with the SNP, having called for broadcasting to be transferred to the control of the Scottish Parliament.

General Election of May 1997

Eventually, John Major could run no further and one of the most anticipated general elections of modern times finally took place on 1 May 1997. As part of a UK-wide landslide victory for Labour, all of Scotland's sitting Conservative MPs were defeated, making reality of the long-held aspiration of a Tory Free Scotland. In Scotland, the 1997 election completed the trend sign-posted by the 1987 election. It confirmed that the despondency felt in 1992 was based on a failure of expectation rather than a Conservative revival.

It was expected that George Robertson would be appointed as Secretary of State for Scotland. He had shadowed the position, had led Labour to a stunning victory in Scotland and was on the record stating that he wished to remain in Scotland, deliver the Parliament and serve as Scotland's first First Minister. There was no doubt, however, that he had been damaged by the political rough and tumble of 1995/96. In wider Scottish society he carried the can for the revisions to the Convention scheme and the referendum affair, or rather the manner in which those changes had been demanded.

Like Robertson, Donald Dewar had a pro-devolution record dating back to the 1970s, and he had led Labour into the Constitutional Convention in 1989 and was greatly respected in Scottish opinion. In 1992, John Smith had rewarded his old friend with a change of political scenery by handing him the Shadow Social Security brief. In 1997, however, Tony Blair asked him to return to Scotland and complete Smith's 'unfinished business'. Dewar returned to Scotland with aides Murray Elder and Wendy Alexander, both of whom had been Labour staffers during the early days of the Convention. They were now re-united to see the project through to its conclusion.

The Referendum Campaign

On 14 May 1997, the legislation providing for the Referendum was introduced, and on the following day 'Scotland Forward', as 'Partners for a Parliament' was now known, was inaugurated. The key question was whether or not the Scottish National Party would join the campaign. Dewar met with SNP Leader Alex Salmond and the Nationalist Parliamentary Leader, Margaret Ewing. They sought assurances that the forthcoming White Paper establishing the Scottish Parliament would not contain a 'glass ceiling', i.e. an explicit prohibition on the Parliament raising the question of independence, e.g. calling a referendum on independence at some time in the future.

Dewar provided the necessary guarantees, which were borne out when the White Paper was published on 24 July 1997. On 27 July the SNP's National Executive endorsed co-operation with 'Scotland Forward', a decision ratified by its National Council of 2 August. With the SNP on board, 'Scotland Forward' was launched on 19 August 1997. 'Scotland Forward's' main problem was not the weakened Tory 'Think Twice' campaign, but noises off stage.[17] In July Labour MP Gordon McMaster died, and the tragic circumstances were still a major talking point among the Scottish media. Their persistent attempts to raise the issue during the 'Scotland Forward' launch left Co-ordinator Paolo Vestri with a difficult job of chairing. The campaign was further disrupted by a second tragedy, the death of Diana, Princess of Wales. In keeping with the mood throughout the United

Kingdom, a cease-fire was called in the referendum campaign. Campaigning resumed on 7 September.

The priority for the CSP was to mobilise its supporters behind 'Scotland Forward'. At grassroots level, CSP members acted as 'Scotland Forward' constituency co-ordinators. At national level, the CSP was represented on the 'Scotland Forward' National Forum by Convener Moira Craig and Isobel Lindsay. The CSP donated £500 to 'Scotland Forward' and printed and distributed a special referendum issue of *Blueprint*. The CSP also made a financial donation to the Common Cause initiative to equip a campaigning vehicle and take the Yes/Yes campaign to every corner of Scotland, particularly the sparsely populated areas.[18]

Despite the weakened state of Scottish Conservatism following the general election wipeout, there was a degree of nervousness in the Yes/Yes campaign. Whether it was the stop/start nature of the campaign, or fear of the supposed Scottish failure of nerve, there was concern that the prize might be denied once again.

According to the BBC's Brian Taylor, Donald Dewar confessed to gloomy moments during the campaign. Apparently Dewar subscribed to the view that it ran counter to modern political thinking to confront the electorate with the potential cost of their decisions. Those comments suggest that Dewar was not a willing partner to the 26 June decision to press for a two question referendum. Dewar's apparent concern about the second question on tax varying seems to have been shared by Tony Blair. When visiting Scotland during the campaign, he expressed to journalists his concern that the second question was in trouble.[19]

Even the most committed home rulers had moments of doubt. During the campaign I acted as the Midlothian co-ordinator for 'Scotland Forward'. As the polls were closing on 11th September, I called the 'Scotland Forward' headquarters in Edinburgh to provide an estimate of the turnout in Midlothian. I reported that the turnout was not as high as hoped, to be told that there was concern over turnout across Scotland.

My concerns were dispelled on arriving at the Midlothian counting centre where the growing piles of Yes votes and the early news from

Clackmannan, the first constituency to declare, indicated that we were on course for a decisive victory. True, a national turnout of 60.4% was disappointing, but it failed to depress the Yes majorities of 74.3% on question 1 and 63.5% on question 2. Three quarters of those who voted supported the establishment of the parliament, while two-thirds voted for the tax varying power. Every constituency voted for a parliament, while only Orkney and Dumfries and Galloway voted against the tax varying provision.[20] It was the expression of what John Smith had described as 'the settled will of the Scottish people'.

CSP: *The Twilight Months*

With an enabling referendum behind it, the Scottish Parliament legislation found fair wind at Westminster. The Scotland Bill was published on 18 December 1997 and received its second reading in early January 1998. Naturally, there was discussion within the CSP as to the future of the organisation post referendum. It was agreed to set a date for the formal dissolution of the CSP, rather than simply allowing it to fade away. It was therefore agreed that once the Scotland Act had received Royal Assent, a Special General Meeting of the CSP would be called to formally dissolve the organisation.

In the eighteen months between the referendum and the dissolution of the CSP, the Campaign was active on the following fronts:

1   Monitoring the progress of the legislation to ensure that key commitments on proportional representation, open government, action on gender balance and vibrant pre-legislative committees were carried through. In part this involved lobbying the Constitutional Steering Group established in November 1997 to devise 'modern', 'accesible', 'open' and 'responsive' government.

2   Ensuring that any ambiguity between the Convention scheme and the emerging legislation was resolved in favour of the spirit of the former, e.g. broadcasting and representation in Europe.

3   Finding a site for the Scottish Parliament building.

4   Fostering active citizenship.[21]

A 'Scottish Six'

Battle lines for a more maximalist home rule future were drawn around the issue of the BBC and the 'Scottish Six'. The BBC's Scottish Broadcasting Council advocated that the main television news broadcast at 6.00pm should be produced in Scotland. The formula of a London produced bulletin of national and international news followed by a Scottish supplement, i.e. *Reporting Scotland*, should be replaced by an integrated hour in which international, British and Scottish news was produced and presented from a distinctively Scottish perspective. If the United Kingdom was decentralising, why not the BBC?

The CSP endorsed the view of the Broadcasting Council and organised a letter writing campaign targeted toward the Reverend Norman Drummond, the BBC National Governor for Scotland, and Sir Christopher Bland, the Chairman of the BBC.[22]

The 'Scottish Six' campaign was unsuccessful in immediate terms but it became a symbol for broadcasting generally, and elevated the question to the top of the list of powers and functions to be considered when the division of responsibilities between Edinburgh and London is reviewed at some future point.

'I don't care if it's situated on the top of Ben Nevis'

Moira Craig's forthright agnosticism on a preferred site for a Scottish Parliament requires to be placed in context. Moira made that comment while the debate for or against a Scottish Parliament was still live, and she was not going to be side tracked from the main debate. Following the referendum, however, the location of the parliament moved centre stage.

From the moment the Callaghan Government purchased the former Royal High School in the late 1970s, to host its Scottish Assembly, the site was widely regarded as the future home of an Assembly or Parliament. For most of its existence the CSA/CSP adapted Thomas Hamilton's portico as its logo. It was not sentiment, however, that led the CSP to prefer the parliament on the hill.

The CSP believed that Calton Hill was both central and accessible. Designed by Thomas Hamilton, the main building on the site is magnificent and an outstanding example of Scotland's built heritage. As the work around the 1991 Jim Boyack Memorial Project had established, there was scope on the site for adaptation and additions in the future, thereby avoiding the massive costs of building on a brown field site.

The CSP's National Secretary, Marion Ralls, was the driving force on this issue. She organised an exhibition featuring the proposed sites at the University of Edinburgh's School of Architecture, in Chambers Street, throughout December 1997. She also organised a well attended public meeting on the issue, chaired by broadcaster Colin Bell, in the Royal Museum of Scotland on 4 December.

Speaking on behalf of the CSP at that meeting, Marion championed Calton Hill's 'potential for phased development', which would produce 'acceptable cost patterns', making it an attractive option both 'politically and practically'.[23] The meeting backed the Royal High School/Calton Hill option but to no avail. A complex new building on the Holyrood site was the eventual choice and the delays and escalating costs have played their part in breeding a degree of public cynicism towards the Parliament.

It is not as if there were no precedents for the situation in which the Donald Dewar-led Scottish Office, and later our MSPs, found themselves in the years 1997-2000.

Like Scotland, Ireland has a historic parliament building, situated on College Green, adjacent to Trinity College. By the time of the granting of Irish independence in 1921/22, however, the building was firmly in the hands of the Bank of Ireland. Other significant buildings with 'parliamentary' associations included the Mansion House, the residence of the Lord Mayor of Dublin. It was in the Round Room of that building that the Sinn Fein majority, elected in the British general election of November 1918, assembled on 21 January 1919 to declare themselves Dail Eireann. Another contender was the University College Dublin's chamber, which had been a venue for debates on the ratification of the Anglo/Irish Treaty in 1922.

As the new Irish Free State was being born, the Provisional Government of W.T. Cosgrave was seeking a home for its Chamber of Deputies (Dail Eireann) and Senators (Seanad Eireann). Plans were made to transform the Royal Hospital, Kilmainham into a parliament house. As the British military slowed its evacuation from that venue, the date for the opening of the two houses of parliament, and the establishment of the Free State, loomed ever nearer. The Lord Mayor and the University College authorities wanted their buildings back, and it was therefore decided to hire the Royal Dublin Society lecture hall, which was part of Leinster House, the town-house of the Earls of Kildare, as a temporary chamber.

By 1924 rising costs led to the abandonment of the Royal Hospital project, and Leinster House was purchased, pending the provision of a purpose built facility at some future date. The favoured sites were a transformed Custom's House, on the banks of the Liffy, and green field sites in Phoenix Park.

Over the intervening decades those plans were rejected in favour of the ongoing renovation and extension of Leinster House. In the year 2000, the latest major refurbishment improved the accommodation for 160 TDs, 60 Senators, the media and parliamentary staff.

Closer to home, Midlothian was among those new district authorities that found the headquarters of predecessor counties and burghs commandeered by the new regional councils, as a result of local government re-organisation in 1975. While Midlothian received 'compensation' from Lothian Region, to finance the building of replacement headquarters, the Midlothian councillors decided against the immediate construction of a new building. They believed that such a course of action could fuel public cynicism, and tarnish the image of the new authority.

Midlothian delayed construction of a new HQ until the late 1980s, and operated from available accommodation across the district until the new Midlothian House opened to little hostile comment in 1992.

There is an interesting CSP postscript relating to the Holyrood building. Following Labour's 1997 victory I was contacted by David Hamilton, younger brother of the Duke of Hamilton and Lord James, and a stalwart CSA/P activist. David told me that historic carved stones from Old Parliament Hall were 'stored' in the grounds of Arniston House in Midlothian, the seat of the Dundas family. David contacted Mrs Dundas Becker regarding the incorporation of those historic stones in a new Parliament building.

David's initial approach was unfruitful and he suggested that I might prompt senior political figures to contact Arniston House. Accordingly, I raised the issue with Secretary of State, Donald Dewar. Today the 'Arniston Stane', which once marked the entrance to Old Parliament Hall, is a favourite feature of the new Holyrood building.

The Scottish Civic Assembly/Forum: A Continuing Role

Until it was dissolved, the Campaign for a Scottish Parliament continued to play a role in the Scottish Civic Assembly, which, as outlined earlier, was a CSP initiative. As originally intended by the CSP, the objects of the continuing Scottish Civic Forum are:

- to provide a route for people and organisations to the early stages of policy making

- to analyse those areas of Scottish life in need of attention and action, and to suggest possible solutions.

- to transmit such recommendations to elected decision makers.

- To provide a degree of scrutiny of draft legislation[24]

Dissolution

The Scotland Act received Royal Assent on 19 November 1998, and in line with decisions taken earlier, that historic event was taken as the cue to dissolve the Campaign for a Scottish Parliament. In the New Year arrangements were made for a Special General Meeting to wind up the affairs of the Campaign. As this was the final act in the life of the CSP, it was agreed to provide extended notice of the meeting to ensure a good turnout. Accordingly, the Special General Meeting eventually took place on Saturday 29 March 1999 in Edinburgh's City Chambers.

From the Chair, Moira Craig regaled us with her own memories of the Campaign, and invited us to contribute some of our own, which several of us did. As far as the business of the meeting was concerned, it was agreed to divide remaining Campaign funds between the Scottish Civic Assembly and Charter 88. It was also agreed that I should write a history of the Campaign. It is a promise now kept.

NOTES AND REFERENCES

[1]   Peter Jones, 'Labour's Referendum Plan: Sell Out or Act of Faith?', in *Scottish Affairs,* No.18, Winter 1997, pp.1-17

[2]   *The Times,* Tuesday 21 May 1996, p.9 and *The Guardian,* 30 May 1996, p.18

[3]   Brian Taylor, *The Scottish Parliament,* Polygon, Edinburgh, 1999, p.71

[4]   Brian Taylor, *The Scottish Parliament,* Polygon, Edinburgh, p.73

[5]   *Ibid,* p.75

[6]   Peter Jones, 'Labour's Referendum Plan: Sell Out or Act of Faith?', in *Scottish Affairs,* No.18, Winter 1997, pp.12-14

[7]   *Ibid*

[8]   *Ibid*

[9]   Kenyon Wright, *The People Say Yes!,* Argyll Publishing, p.245

[10] *Ibid,* p.250

[11] CSP. Schedule of CSP/Charter 88 joint meetings in Edinburgh and Glasgow 1995/1996

[12] CSP. Minutes of the Annual General Meeting, held on 20 April 1996

[13] CSP. Minutes of the National Executive Committee meeting, held on 18 September 1996

[14] CSP. Minutes of the National Executive Committee meeting, held on 16 October 1996

[15] Kenyon Wright, *The People Say Yes!,* Argyll Publishing, 1997, p.259

[16] Nigel Smith, 'The Business Case of Devolution', in *Scottish Affairs,* No.16, Summer 1996. pp.7-17

[17] Peter Jones, 'A Start to a New Song: The 1997 Devolution Referendum', in *Scottish Affairs,* No.21, Autumn 1997, pp.1-16

[18] CSP. *Campaign*, Edinburgh, August 1997

[19] Brian Taylor, *The Scottish Parliament*, Polygon, Edinburgh, 1999, p.135

[20] *Ibid*, p.138

[21] CSP. 'After the Referendum. Whither the CSP?'
www.cybersurf.co.uk/cscoparl/whither

[22] CSP. 'The BBC Six O'Clock News'
www.cybersurf.co.uk/cscoparl/bbc-news

[23] CSP. 'Calton Hill. The Capital Site for Scotland's Parliament'
www.cybersurf.co.uk/cscoparl/building

[24] CSP. 'The Scottish Civic Assembly'
www.cybersurf.co.uk/cscoparl/sca

CONCLUSION

The Legacy of the CSA/CSP

Tae See Oorsels as Ithers See Us

'The CSA had been formed by Labour home rulers, notably Jim Boyack, who held no position of any significance in the party, and a few Nationalists who had not been too scarred by 1979. Its object was not just to keep the flame alive but to try and get rival politicians to warm themselves around it. It was thus the inheritor of the home rule 'movement' tendency which had vanished with John MacCormick.'

Christopher Harvie and Peter Jones, *The Road to Home Rule*, Polygon, Edinburgh, 2000, p.147

'... the Campaign for a Scottish Assembly was gently assembling support for a consensual approach, urging that the path to change lay in reasonable people working together. Nothing is more difficult for a politician to reject than polite reason, particularly when accompanied by phrases like 'the will of the people'.'

Brian Taylor, *The Scottish Parliament*, Polygon, Edinburgh, 1999, p.37

'The CSA, lacking its own national organisation and a large membership list, was using a certain amount of ventriloquism to persuade the big parties to take its ideas seriously. But it worked.'

Andrew Marr, *The Battle for Scotland*, Penguin, London, 1992, p.198

READERS WILL MAKE THEIR own evaluation of the contribution of the Campaign for a Scottish Assembly/Campaign for a Scottish Parliament to the achievement of Scottish home rule. Any fair and informed observer of Scottish politics from 1980-1999 could not deny the CSA/P's role in keeping the home rule flame burning during the difficult years from 1980 to1983. Later, from 1987 to 1990, the CSA/P was pivotal in prompting 'A Claim of Right for Scotland' and the Scottish Constitutional Convention which flowed from it.

It can be argued that, following eighteen years in opposition, any incoming Labour government would have introduced home rule, with or without the efforts of the CSA/CSP, the Claim of Right, the Constitutional Convention or any other pressure group. I have already acknowledged that Margaret Thatcher, her ideology and style, was a major recruiting sergeant for the home rule cause during the 1980s. Her determination to impose the detested Poll Tax, in the years 1988-90, marked the high water mark of Scottish resistance.

While accepting the effective, if unwitting, contribution of Thatcher's Conservatives to raising Scottish sentiment, and the likelihood of a Labour government delivering on home rule, I would argue that the Scottish Parliament, and our new constitutional settlement, bears the stamp of the CSA/CSP in a number of respects.

Powers

CSA veterans well remembered the torturous Westminster process that produced the 1978 legislation. By the very nature of the organisation, those involved in the CSA/CSP tended to favour a 'maximalist' home rule scheme. The CSA/CSP argued that the establishing legislation should list the powers reserved to Westminster, and that all other areas should be regarded as being within the competency of the Scottish Parliament.[1] This was the approach taken in the Government of Ireland Act of 1920. The Constitutional Convention shared the CSA/CSP's enthusiasm for that model, and the Scotland Act was constructed along those lines.

Back in July 1998, however, there were few observers who spotted the significance of obscure House of Lords debates, and a series of Devolution Guidance Notes, which underpin what has come to be known as the 'Sewel Motion' procedure. Named after the former Aberdeen University academic and government minister, this convention was devised to prevent Westminster exercising its sovereign right to legislate for Scotland, on any issue, without gaining the consent of the Scottish Parliament. While the convention was designed to protect the authority of the Scottish Parliament, it has become a route for devolving back to Westminster the right to legislate for Scotland on a series of measures. It began with the Fireworks Bill in the summer of 2003, and at the time of writing in summer 2004 the device has been used on almost forty occasions. They include instances of what might be considered as socially sensitive legislation, e.g. same-sex unions.

Devolution should be about taking responsibility, not passing the buck.

Procedures

The Constitutional Convention argued strongly that the Scottish Parliament should be free from Executive domination and called for clear channels of accountability and scrutiny. To that end the Scottish Parliament has established standing, pre-legislative committees with the power to initiate legislation. The Parliament's Petitions Committee is widely recognised as a democratic departure.

As outlined earlier, the Scottish Civic Forum, a creation of the CSA/CSP, continues to provide Scottish civic society with an access route into the legislative process.

Representation

Following the debacle of the 1979 referendum it was clear to any serious home ruler that any new Scottish legislature must be elected by proportional representation. Support for fair votes was essential in transforming the call for home rule from a party political proposal to a Scottish national demand. The CSA/CSP recognised this from its inception. Over the course of the next twenty years the organisation held workshops and conferences, and produced publications, as a contribution to creating a consensus in favour of a system that would allocate seats in a Scottish Parliament according to the parties' share of the popular vote. Cynics, whether Conservatives or commentators, maintained that agreement would never be achieved on the issue. Malcolm Rifkind was so convinced that he threatened to jump off the roof of St Andrews House if the Convention parties agreed on a proportional scheme. Another Tory broken promise! The key decision, taken by Labour in Dunoon in March 1990, was greeted as a 'political earthquake'.

While the Convention failed to reach agreement on a statutory method of ensuring the equal representation of men and women, the years of debate around '50:50' created a political climate which has resulted in the Scottish Parliament containing an internationally unprecedented high percentage of women legislators. There is no doubt that senior women in the CSA/CSP made an important contribution to that end.

People

A number of MSPs, past and present, were involved in the CSA/CSP to different degrees prior to serving the Scottish Parliament. They include Sarah Boyack, Pauline MacNeill, Mike Watson, John McAllion, Frank McAveety, Donald Gorrie, Dennis Canavan, Robin Harper and Jack McConnell. The involvement of these key figures in the CSA/CSP may have assisted in oiling the wheels of consensual working and coalition building.[2]

A Blythsom End Tae an Auld Sang

The demand for changes to the incorporating Union of 1707 is as old as the Union itself. From the beginnings of mass democratic politics in the 1880s, the demand for home rule has been a consistent feature of the Scottish political landscape. On several occasions in the past 120 years it has given rise to movements which cut across party divides: the original Scottish Home Rule Association of the 1880s and '90s, the reformed Scottish Home Rule Association of the 1920s and the Covenant movement of the late 1940s/early '50s. While each of these campaigns and movements influenced Scottish politics, they ultimately failed to secure their objectives and faded into oblivion.

Those of us who were involved with the Campaign for a Scottish Assembly/Parliament of the 1980s and '90s saw the orderly dissolution of our organisation following the achievement of its objective.

It was a privilege to be involved.

NOTES AND REFERENCES

1   See Andrew Burns in Hassan, Gerry (ed.), *A Guide to the Scottish Parliament*, Stationery Office, Edinburgh, 1999, pp.43-48
2   Mike Watson, *Year Zero: An Inside View of the Scottish Parliament, Edinburgh*, Polygon, Edinburgh, 2001, p.5

CSA/CSP Chronology

1 March 1979	Despite receiving the support of 51.6% of those who voted, the Callaghan Government's devolution proposals are defeated in a referendum.
Autumn 1979	Home rule enthusiasts re-group.
1 March 1980	Campaign for a Scottish Assembly (CSA) formed.
6 March 1980	Glasgow Branch of the CSA established.
April 1980	CSA holds first ever 'fringe meeting', at the STUC in Perth.
June 1980	CSA active around the Glasgow Central by election.
28 June 1980	CSA Edinburgh Branch organises the 'Festival of the People' on Calton Hill.
29 November 1980	CSA Constitution adopted by a national meeting held in Glasgow.
30 November 1980	CSA Glasgow Branch organises 'St Andrews Day Festival of the People'.
28 March 1981	CSA holds its first National Convention.
June 1981	CSA successfully calls on the Monopoly and Mergers to take evidence in Scotland on the proposed merger of the Royal Bank of Scotland Standard and Charter.
October 1981	CSA publishes *Blue Print*.
15 February 1982	CSA seizes on the first ever meeting of the Scottish Grand Committee, in Scotland, to highlight the democratic deficit.
March 1982	CSA campaigns around Glasgow Hillhead by election.
20 March 1982	CSA stages its second National Convention.
8 September 1982	CSA launches attack on government social and economic policy.

11 December 1982	Jim Boyack succeeds Jack Brand as CSA National Chairman.
15 February 1983	CSA stages first Westminster lobby.
March 1983	CSA opens office in Edinburgh.
9 April 1983	CSA holds its third National Convention.
June 1983	CSA campaigns around the general election.
9 July 1983	CSA responds to general election result with an Agenda Conference.
August 1983	CSA calls for 'islands devolution' at the Montgomery Committee.
17 September 1983	CSA holds a recall National Convention. The proposal for a Constitutional Convention becomes top priority.
January 1984	CSA establishes Inter Party Forum to build support for the Convention.
Feb/March 1984	CSA stages Referendum 5th Anniversary Week of Action.
28 February 1984	CSA launches draft proposals for a Constitutional Convention.
1 March 1984	The Labour Party launches its 'Green Paper' on Devolution.
1 March 1984	CSA stages all night vigil outside the Royal High School, the intended site for a Scottish Parliament.
June 1984	Jim Ross makes the CSA his political priority.
September 1984	Constitutional Convention becomes SNP policy.
13 October 1984	CSA AGM re-structures the campaign, the term 'Convener' replaces 'chairman'.
24 November 1984	CSA launches Local Government initiative.
November 1984	The CSA includes Assembly question in Systems3 opinion survey.
2 March 1985	CSA organises 'Towards a Constitutional Convention' as a launch pad for proposals on the membership and remit of a Constitutional Convention.
16 May 1985	CSA Convention proposals are circulated.

July 1985	CSA opens dialogue with the North East of England TUC.
January 1986	Campbell Christie takes over as General Secretary of the STUC.
January 1986	Jim Ross collects 'Scot of the Year Award' for his efforts to prevent the privatisation of the Trustees Savings Bank.
January to June 1986	CSA undertakes the 'Agreeing an Assembly' process.
1 March 1986	'Youth for an Assembly' event.
14 March 1986	CSA organises 'Model Assembly' exercise in Strathclyde Region's debating chamber.
November 1986	CSA launches business initiative.
27 November 1986	Canon Kenyon Wright emerges as the star speaker at the CSA's Declaration Dinner.
March 1987	CSA rejects call for tactical voting.
May/June 1987	CSA runs newspaper advertising during the 1987 general election.
June 1987	Scottish politics rocked by reduction in the number of Scottish Tory MPs, from 22 to 10. The term 'Doomsday Scenario' is coined.
20 June 1987	CSA holds Special National Council to respond to the general election result.
July 1987	CSA launches a review of its structures and finances.
September 1987	CSA supports STUC organised 'Festival for Scottish Democracy'.
28 November 1987	CSA endorses internal reforms.
February 1988	Alan Armstrong replaces Jim Boyack as CSA Convener.
11 February 1988	CSA launches the Constitutional Steering Committee with Sir Robert Grieve in the Chair and Jim Ross as Secretary.
April 1988	Increased funding stream enables CSA to open an office and employ a part-time worker.
11 June 1988	CSA members leaflet Tory-held constituencies on Democracy Day.

13 July 1988	Constitutional Steering Committee reports. 'A Claim of Right for Scotland' is published.
October 1988	Donald Dewar indicates that Labour might join a Constitutional Convention.
10 November 1988	The SNP's Jim Sillars wins the Glasgow Govan by election.
12 November 1988	Labour's Scottish Executive agrees to participate in the Convention process.
27 January 1989	CSA meets with representatives of Labour, SNP, Liberal Democrats, the Convention of Scottish Local Authorities, the STUC and the Scottish Council of Churches to discuss the Convention proposal.
11 February 1989	SNP National Executive votes against participating in the proposed Constitutional Convention.
4 March 1989	SNP National Assembly backs its Executive's position.
30 March 1989	First meeting of the Scottish Constitutional Convention.
December 1989	CSA organises fact finding Convention delegation to the Basque country.
6/7 January 1990	CSA joins with the Campaign for a Welsh Assembly, and Charter 88, in organising 'The 1990s, a Decade of Constitutional Change', at Coleg Harlech.
March 1990	Isobel Lindsay succeeds Alan Armstrong as Convener.
10 March 1990	Labour's Scottish Conference accepts the principle of proportional representation in elections for a Scottish Parliament.
14 July 1990	CSA supports 'The Day for Scotland' in Stirling.
September 1990	Harry Conroy appointed as Constitutional Convention Campaign Director, a post partly financed by the CSA.

30 November 1990	The Scottish Constitutional Convention presents its first report, 'Towards Scotland's Parliament'.
December 1990	Margaret Thatcher ousted. John Major takes over as Prime Minister.
1991	CSA members at the forefront of the Convention Campaign, distributing tabloid newspaper, leaflets and campaign postcards.
1991	CSA organises and delivers the Jim Boyack Memorial Project.
February/April 1992	CSA support for tactical voting in the general election leads to legal threat.
April 1992	CSA welcomes the new home rule pressure groups created as a reaction to the Conservative victory in the general election.
October 1992	The organisation is renamed Campaign for a Scottish Parliament (CSP).
18 November 1992	Differences over CSP strategy result in the resignation of key officers.
12 December 1992	CSP involved in the organisation of 'Scotland demands Democracy' demonstration targeted at the European Heads of Government meeting in Edinburgh.
March 1993	CSP supports STUC proposal that the civic organisations involved in the December demonstration should co-ordinate their efforts as the Coalition for Scottish Democracy (CSD).
March 1993	Moira Craig succeeds Isobel Lindsay as CSP Convener.
April 1993	The Constitutional Convention appoints a Constitutional Commission to address issues glossed over in 'Towards Scotland's Parliament'.
December 1993	CSP involved in the organisation of the Falkirk Referendum.

December 1993	CSP represented on CSD delegation to European Parliament.
December 1993	Court of Session rules that local authority contributions to the Constitutional Convention, via the CSP, are within the law.
January 1994	CSP endorses the idea of a Scottish Civic Assembly.
18 June 1994	Consultative conference establishes the Scottish Civic Assembly.
July 1994	CSP publishes 'Campaigners' Pack'.
10 August 1994	CSP meets with the Constitutional Commission.
October 1994	Constitutional Commission presents its report.
29 October 1994	CSP autumn conference pronounces the Constitutional Commission's report a missed opportunity.
December 1994	Constitutional Convention launches 'Preparing for Change Project'.
10-12 February 1995	CSP hosts 'Hands Across the Borders' seminar.
May 1995	Labour revisits elements of 'Towards Scotland's Parliament'.
30 November 1995	The revised Constitutional Convention scheme, 'Scotland's Parliament, Scotland's Right', is launched.
April 1996	CSP publishes 'Blue Print', a popular guide to the Scottish home rule question and the Constitutional Convention scheme.
June 1996	Labour commits itself to a pre-legislative referendum on the Constitutional Convention Scheme with a second, specific question on the proposed tax-varying power.
October 1996	CSP member, Nigel Smith addresses the organisation of the pro-home rule campaign in the proposed referendum.

1 May 1997	General election landslide returns Labour to office and buries Scots Tories.
14 May 1997	'Scotland Forward' established.
May 1997	CSP agrees major donation to 'Scotland Forward', and to produce a referendum special issue of 'Blue Print'.
24 July 1997	Scottish Parliament White Paper published.
July/August 1997	The deaths of Gordon McMaster MP, and Diana, Princess of Wales, overshadow the early days of the referendum campaign.
2 August 1997	SNP confirms involvement in 'Scotland Forward'.
11 September 1997	Referendum. 74.3% support the establishment of a Scottish Parliament. 63.5% vote for the tax varying power.
November 1997	Donald Dewar establishes the Constitutional Steering Group (CSG).
December 1997	CSP National Secretary, Marian Ralls, plays a prominent part in the debate around the location of a new Scottish Parliament building.
18 December 1997	Scotland Bill published.
12 January 1998	Scotland Bill begins its Second Reading.
January 1998	CSG publishes its report.
January 1998	CSP agrees to dissolve following the Scotland Act receiving Royal Assent.
1998	CSP members continue to monitor the legislative process, campaign on the site for the parliament building and argue for the creation of a 'Scottish Six'.
19 November 1998	Scotland Act receives Royal Assent.
29 March 1999	Special Annual General Meeting in Edinburgh's City Chambers dissolves the Campaign for a Scottish Parliament.

Bibliography

Primary Sources

CSA/CSP Sources

Annual General Meeting minutes and papers
National Conference minutes and papers
National Convention minutes and papers
National Executive Committee minutes and papers
National Committee minutes and papers
Policy documents
Publications
Leaflets
Submissions
Newsletters
Edinburgh Branch papers
Glasgow Branch papers
Helensburgh Branch papers

The papers and publications of the following organisations were also consulted:

Scottish Home Rule Association (1918-1929)
Scottish Convention (1942)
Scottish Covenant Association (1950)
Scottish National Assembly (1947-1953)
Yes for Scotland (1979)
Constitutional Steering Committee (1988)
Scottish Constitutional Convention (1989-1997)
Scotland Forward (1997)

Periodicals

Crann Tara
Radical Scotland
Scottish Government Yearbook

Scottish Affairs
Scottish Historical Review

Newspapers

Daily Record
The Herald (formerly *Glasgow Herald*)
Scotsman
Scotland on Sunday
Sunday Standard

Secondary Sources

Bochel, J.M., Denver, David T. and Allan Macartney
The Referendum Experience, Scotland 1979, Aberdeen University Press, Aberdeen, 1981

Brand, Jack
National Movement in Scotland, Routledge, London, 1978

Clements, Alan, Farquharson, Kenny and Wark, Kirsty
Restless Nation, Mainstream, Edinburgh, 1996

Donnachie, Iain *et al*,
Forward! Labour Politics in Scotland, 1888-1988, Polygon, Edinburgh, 1988

Edwards, Owen Dudley (ed)
Claim of Right for Scotland, Polygon, Edinburgh, 1988

Drucker, Henry
Breakaway, The Scottish Labour Party, Edinburgh University Student Publications Board, Edinburgh, 1978

Galbraith, Russell
Without Quarter: A Biography of Tom Johnston, Mainstream, Edinburgh, 1995

Gollan, John
Scottish Prospect: An Economic, Administrative and Social Survey, Communist Party of Great Britain, 1948

Harvie, Christopher
Scotland and Nationalism, Revised Edition, Routledge, London, 1997

Hassan, Gerry (ed)
A Guide to the Scottish Parliament Stationery Office, Edinburgh, 1999

Harvie, Christopher and Jones, Peter
The Road to Home Rule, Polygon, Edinburgh, 2000

Keating, Michael and Bleiman, David
Labour and Scottish Nationalism, Macmillan, London, 1979

Knox, William
Scottish Labour Leaders 1920-1950, Mainstream, Edinburgh, 1983

MacCormick, John
The Flag in the Wind, Gollancz, 1955

McLean, Robert
Labour and Scottish Home Rule, Parts 1 and 2, Scottish Labour Action, Whitburn, 1990/91

Marr, Andrew
The Battle for Scotland, Penguin, London, 1992

Mitchell, James
Strategies for Self-Government. The Campaigns for a Scottish Parliament, Edinburgh University Press, Edinburgh, 1996

Sillars, Jim
Scotland: A Case for Optimism, Polygon, Edinburgh, 1986

Smout, T.C.
A Century of the Scottish People 1830-1950, Collins, Glasgow, 1986

Taylor, Brian
The Scottish Parliament, Polygon, Edinburgh, 1999

Watson, Mike
Year Zero: An Inside View of the Scottish Parliament, Polygon, Edinburgh, 2001

Wright, Kenyon
The People Say Yes!, Argyll, Colintraive, 1998

Index

Some other books published by **LUATH** PRESS

published from Scotland, read around the world

Scotlands of the Mind

Angus Calder
ISBN 1 84282 008 7 PB £9.99

Does Scotland as a 'nation' have any real existence? In Britain, in Europe, in the World? Or are there a multitude of multiform 'Scot-lands of the Mind'?

These soul-searching questions are probed in this timely book by prize-winning author and journalist, Angus Calder. Informed and intelligent, this new volume presents the author at his thought-provoking best. The absorbing journey through many possible Scotlands – fictionalised, idealised, and politicised – is sure to fascinate.

This perceptive and often highly personal writing shows the breathtaking scope of Calder's analytical power. Fact or fiction, individual or international, politics or poetry, statistics or statehood, no subject is taboo in a volume that offers an overview of the vicissitudes and changing nature of Scottishness.

Through mythical times to manufactured histories, from Empire and Diaspora, from John Knox to Home Rule and beyond, Calder shatters literary, historical and cultural misconceptions and provides invaluable insights into the Scottish psyche. Offering a fresh understanding of an ever-evolving Scotland, *Scotlands of the Mind* contributes to what Calder himself has called 'the needful getting of a new act together'.

Thoughtful and provocative, Calder is among the best essayists of today.
Bernard Crick, THE GUARDIAN

Angus Calder has proved himself one of the most sophisticated thinkers and writers on the gleaming new Scotland.
THE SCOTSMAN

Building a Nation

Post Devolution Nationalism in Scotland
Viewpoints [series]
Kenny MacAskill
ISBN 1 84282 081 8 PB £4.99

'Where stands Scotland post Devolution and what is the future for Nationalism in a devolved Parliament? Is the Scottish Parliament a Union-ist dead end or a Nationalist Highway to Independence? Has Devolution killed the SNP stone dead or given it a platform to build from? These are questions that need answered as Scotland begins to come to terms with Devolution and decides where and whether to go next'.
KENNY MacASKILL

In this book, Kenny MacAskill searches for the answers to these questions, vital to the future of 'the best small nation in the world'. He makes the case for a distinctive Scottish version of social democracy that can balance a vibrant economy with quality public services, and believes that Post Devolution Nationalism is about Building a Nation to be proud of.

This book is an important, possibly seminal, contribution to a debate that reflects on the meaning of independence, not just in terms of its constitutional-legal meanings but its wider meanings. It is challenging and provocative in the very best sense. There is an underlying and powerful message of optimism, a quiet self-confidence which challenges what Kenny MacAskill calls the 'outward swagger but huge inner self-doubt'. The book may be primarily addressed to a Nationalist audience but should be read well beyond supporters of constitutional independence.
PROFESSOR JAMES MITCHELL,
DEPARTMENT OF GOVERNMENT,
UNIVERSITY OF STRATHCLYDE

A timely intervention for a party entering a critical phase in its history... a manifesto to inspire and infuriate; pacey, intelligent and accessible. Like all good political pamphlets it is best enjoyed when read out loud.
SCOTTISH REVIEW OF BOOKS

Old Scotland New Scotland

Jeff Fallow

ISBN 0 946487 40 5 PB £6.99

Together we can build a new Scotland based on Labour's values.
DONALD DEWAR, Party Political Broadcast

Despite the efforts of decent Mr Dewar, the voters may yet conclude they are looking at the same old hacks in brand new suits.
IAN BELL, THE INDEPENDENT

At times like this you suddenly realise how dangerous the neglect of Scottish history in our schools and universities may turn out to be.
MICHAEL FRY, THE HERALD

...one of the things I hope will go is our chip on the shoulder about the English... The SNP has a huge responsibility to articulate Scottish independence in a way that is pro-Scottish and not anti-English.
ALEX SALMOND, THE SCOTSMAN

Scottish politics have never been more exciting. In *Old Scotland New Scotland* Jeff Fallow takes us on a graphic voyage through Scotland's turbulent history, from earliest times through to the present day and beyond. This fast-track guide is the quick way to learn what your history teacher didn't tell you, essential reading for all who seek an understanding of Scotland and its history.

Eschewing the romanticisation of his country's past, Fallow offers a new perspective on an old nation.

Too many people associate Scottish history with tartan trivia or outworn romantic myth. This book aims to blast that stubborn idea.
JEFF FALLOW

Eurovision or American Dream? Britain, the Euro and the Future of Europe

David Purdy

ISBN 1 84282 036 2 PB £3.99

Should Britain join the euro?
Where is the European Union going?
Must America rule the world?

Eurovision or American Dream? assesses New Labour's prevarications over the euro and the EU's deliberations about its future against the background of transatlantic discord. Highlighting the contrasts between European social capitalism and American free market individualism, David Purdy shows how Old Europe's

welfare states can be renewed in the age of the global market. This, he argues, is essential if European governments are to reconnect with their citizens and revive enthusiasm for the European project. It would also enable the EU to challenge US hegemony, not by transforming itself into a rival superpower, but by championing an alternative model of social development and changing the rules of the global game.

In this timely and important book David Purdy explains why joining the euro is not just a question of economics, but a question about the future political direction of Britain and its place in Europe.
PROFESSOR ANDREW GAMBLE, DIRECTOR, POLITICAL ECONOMY RESEARCH CENTRE, DEPARTMENT OF POLITICS, UNIVERSITY OF SHEFFIELD

Scotland – Land and Power the agenda for land reform

Andy Wightman
in association with
Democratic Left Scotland
foreword by Lesley Riddoch

ISBN 0 946487 70 7 PB £5.00

What is land reform?
Why is it needed?
Will the Scottish Parliament really make a difference?

Scotland – Land and Power argues passionately that nothing less than a radical, comprehensive programme of land reform can make the difference that is needed. Now is no time for palliative solutions which treat the symptoms and not the causes.

Scotland – Land and Power is a controversial and provocative book that clarifies the complexities of landownership in Scotland. Andy Wightman explodes the myth that land issues are relevant only to the far flung fringes of rural Scotland, and questions mainstream political commitment to land reform. He presents his own far-reaching programme for change and a pragmatic, inspiring vision of how Scotland can move from outmoded, unjust power structures towards a more equitable landowning democracy.

Writers like Andy Wightman are determined to make sure that the hurt of the last century is not compounded by a rushed solution in the next. This accessible, comprehensive but passionately argued book is quite simply essential reading and perfectly timed – here's hoping Scotland's legislators agree.
LESLEY RIDDOCH

Trident on Trial: the case for people's disarmament

Angie Zelter

ISBN 1 84282 004 4   PB   £9.99

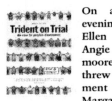

On a beautiful summer's evening in 1999, three women – Ellen Moxley, Ulla Roder and Angie Zelter – boarded a barge moored on a Scottish loch and threw some computer equipment overboard. Sheriff Margaret Gimblett acquitted 'The Trident Three' on the basis that they were acting as global citizens preventing nuclear crime. This led to what is thought to be the world's first High Court examination of the legality of an individual state's deployment of nuclear weapons...

Is Trident inherently unlawful and immoral?

When can a state use or threaten to use nuclear weapons?

Should international law take precedence over a sovereign government's?

Can a government be held accountable for ownership of weapons of mass destruction?

When is a citizen justified in acting against what she reasonably believes to be Government crime?

Is whose name does the UK government deploy 144 nuclear warheads, each around 10 times the power of that dropped on Hiroshima killing some 150,000 people?

This is Angie's personal account of the campaign. It also includes profiles of and contributions by some of the people and groups who have pledged to prevent nuclear crime in peaceful and practical ways. Without such public pressure governments will not abide by the Advisory Opinion nor implement their international agreements to abolish nuclear weapons.

This fine book should be read by everyone, especially those who have the slightest doubt that the world will one day be rid of nuclear weapons.
JOHN PILGER

Reading this book will help you play your part in keeping human life human.
REV DR ANDREW MacLELLAN, MODERATOR OF THE GENERAL ASSEMBLY OF THE CHURCH OF SCOTLAND 2000/2001

A Passion for Scotland

David R. Ross

ISBN 1 84282 019 2   PB   £5.99

David R. Ross is passionate about Scotland's past. And its future. In this heartfelt journey through Scotland's story, he shares his passion for what it means to be a Scot.

Eschewing xenophobia, his deep understanding of how Scotland's history touches her people shines through. All over Scotland, into England and Europe, over to Canada, and the United States – the people and the places that bring Scotland's story to life and death, are here. Included are the:

- Early Scots
- Wallace and Bruce
- The Union
- Montrose
- The Jacobites
- John MacLean
- Tartan Day USA

and, revealed for the first time, the burial places of all Scotland's monarchs.

This is not a history book, but it covers history.

This is not a travel guide, but some places mentioned might be worth a visit.

This is not a political manifesto, but a personal one.

Read this book to discover your roots and your passion for Scotland.

The biker-historian's unique combination of unabashed romanticism and easy irreverence make him the ideal guide to historical subjects all too easily swallowed up in maudlin sentiment or 'demythologised' by academic studies.
THE SCOTSMAN

Ross's patriotism is straightforward and unquestioning, albeit relieved by a pawky sense of humour.
THE HERALD